AMERICAN DREAM
...OR NIGHTMARE?

BY OMAR MESSINA

DORRANCE
PUBLISHING CO
EST. 1920
PITTSBURGH, PENNSYLVANIA 15238

Dorrance Publishing Co
585 Alpha Drive
Pittsburgh, PA 15238
Visit our website at *www.dorrancebookstore.com*

ISBN: 978-1-6491-3369-4
eISBN: 978-1-6491-3597-1

AMERICAN DREAM

...OR NIGHTMARE?

Myself a year old at my maternal grandparents' house in Guadalajara

My life has been in a constant state of movement ever since I can remember. I never know when I'm going to be grounded and lead a normal life. As far as I can remember, my earliest memory is living in Mexico. I was born October 22, 1980 in a hospital in the city of Zapopan next to Guadalajara, Jalisco where we resided. We lived on 2027 Hacienda la Llave in the neighborhood of Arandas in Guadalajara, Jalisco. My father got a job offered as a Spanish teacher in New Orleans, Louisiana in the United States in the summer of 1987 when my father was only twenty-seven years old, and I was six years old at the time. He was one of three hundred teachers selected in Mexico to teach in the United States for a job program offered by the two governments. A few years ago, my mother told me they gave my dad the option to either go to the States or go to China, and my father chose the states to be closer to Mexico. I was dumbfounded when she told me China; my life would've been a lot different if I would've been raised in the orient. In New Orleans is where I would learn English, and as a six-year-old, you're like a sponge, and I would absorb it quickly to the point as if it were my first language.

Ruber (two years old) and myself (seven years old) at our New Orleans, Louisiana apartment after school trying to entertain ourselves with toys.

The two years we lived there, thanks to the teacher program, there were also other teachers and their families who came, and we started to hang out so much it felt like we were back home. We lived next to a neighborhood in the States called "the projects" where it was predominantly African American. My dad worked as a teacher in the daytime and as a waiter at a prestigious restaurant at night. My brother Ruber and I weren't allowed to go outside unless my dad was there, and my mom didn't know how to drive, so we just hung out at home and entertained ourselves with whatever we could.

At school I felt lost without friends and scared. The school was about 85 percent African American, and in Guadalajara there were no blacks, so it was a new environment I had to get accustomed to. I would get into fights every day for two reasons: one, they didn't like me because I wasn't black and two, I didn't know English that well, so as a kid growing up in this hostile environment, I began to have a hatred towards anyone who was black—which later in life I would overcome thanks to the social skills I would develop. Whenever my dad would have some time off from his two jobs, they would take us to the French Quarter and Bourbon Street or to the Super Dome, and sometimes we would take a ferry that would cross the Mississippi River and were amazed the ferry could carry even your car too.

My dad taking the picture of my mom, Ruber and myself overlooking the Mississippi River by the ferry docks in New Orleans, Louisiana.

When the job permit ended and it was time to go back to Mexico, instead of figuring out a way to apply for a resident card or stay in the US, my dad decided to take us back to Mexico in the fall of 1988. For me it was a relief, back to my friends, no more fighting because I was different, no more fighting because of the language barrier, it was great. the same year my paternal grandfather would pass away. I remember him being a tall man whom everybody adored and had a personality that carried with him and made everybody respect him. He had fourteen children, my father being the eleventh in line of the Messina Reyes blood line.

Ignacio Messina Peña my paternal grandfather at approximate age of 40 taken in his home town of Colima in Mexico

Before we left to Louisiana, I had done kindergarten and first grade in Mexico then going to second and third in New Orleans, coming back to start fourth grade in Mexico. Math as universal as it is in the academic world across the globe was the only subject that didn't change, and yet I was behind even though it remains my favorite subject to this day. Mexican math was about two years more advanced than in the United States back in the 1980's, and in fourth grade I had to know square root already and long division. Where in the States by third grade, I was still learning how to add and subtract.

I had uncles like so many undocumented immigrants in the 1980s who, thanks to the Ronald Reagan administration, were able to adjust their legal status in the United States by immigration reform passed by congress and signed by the president on November 6 of 1986. My dad would've been part of that wave but declined because he didn't picture himself living far away from his family in Mexico and didn't see himself living abroad. When some of my uncles asked him to start his paperwork, he declined the offer.

It was now 1989, and we were living back in our house in Hacienda la Llave and my dad began noticing after some time that it's not the same making pesos and making dollars. He had to have three jobs to support a family of four to make ends meet. It took me awhile to adapt to school again because the school system is somewhat. different.

In the United States, schools provide everything a student needs, and I was amazed students failed because in Mexico you have to bring your own pencil, paper, buy your own book, kind of like college, and they expect everything you do to be perfect. One thing I always remember is you could put math, science, and history all in one page, and in Mexico you had to have it in separate paper, and if the teacher didn't understand it, you had to perfect your writing skills or they wouldn't accept your homework.

In the US in math, for example, I would get ten to fifteen problems and that's it. You would do them and give them to the teacher the next day and in Mexico you had to write 5, 10, 15, 20, 25… etc etc all the way to 5,000 with a pencil. I literally had finger cramps when I did homework and also left a mark on my finger for the next two weeks; some nights I couldn't even go out to play because I spent all afternoon doing homework. The following year as I was in the middle of fifth grade, my dad decided we would all move to California to follow the American dream.

On the day my youngest brother Jonathan was to be born, my younger brother Ruber and I along with my dad were walking around in circles outside the hospital thinking of a name, In Mexico when a baby is being born, nobody but the doctor and a few nurses are allowed to be in the delivery room. My dad would ask us for an idea, but I stared at him with a blank face and my brother Ruber yells "cebolla," which means onion in Spanish. My dad and I stared at him like he was an idiot but decided to laugh about it because it would be idiotic to name a kid onion, then again in today's world anything can happen.

My brother Jonathan Messina was born July 5, 1990, two weeks before my brother Ruber would turn five years old. For the longest time I would take care of him not like a brother, but like my own child. I was so proud of him I didn't let a single fly get near him; if it even thought of getting near him, I would be on that fly like white on rice. I would tear it up into a million pieces to let everybody know I wasn't going to let anything happen to my little brother. Funnily enough in his early years he was afraid of flies. I guess I should've let one get on him.

My dad left in October of 1990 to the San Francisco Bay Area to find a place for us to live and to find work while we left our house and went to go live with my maternal grandparents. On December 16, 1990 we left the Guadalajara international airport and arrived at the San Francisco, California international airport where my dad awaited anxiously. We would stay in the apartments by Vineyard Avenue in Pleasanton with my aunt, Licho, who was my dad's sister and fourth in line of my paternal grandmothers fourteen kids. My aunt, her two kids Marco and Alicia, and us—a family of five—shared a two-bedroom townhouse apartment for a while until both families had enough to branch on our own.

My mom Alicia with long-time friend Maria Rios in one of her birthday parties, celebrating it at a friend's house in Livermore, California in 1992.

My dad found a job at Home Depot while my mom worked at the military base Camp in Dublin, California as a cook for about 500 Army soldiers on any given day. It's where my mom would meet her friends Maria Rios and Sylvia Jiminez. Maria Rios still keeps in contact with my mom, and to this day they remain good friends and has pledged her unconditional help.

In Pleasanton is where I would finish elementary and middle school. I went to Fairland Flyers Elementary, then on to Pleasanton Middle Schools three years before heading off to Amador High School in 1994. During middle school, I met the closest friends I had for those three years, which were Miguel Anaya from El Salvador, Nery Castillo from Mexico City, Claudio Solorio from Sonora, Mexico, and Andy Cano from Colombia. Us five were practically the only Spanish-speaking kids in the whole school and began to hang out more and more since we were all in the ESL program (English as a Second Language).

In this school, since it was about 90 percent Caucasian, is where I would be bullied a second time and this time by Caucasian kids. The type of bullying was different from when I lived in New Orleans, and I would get beat up. This time it was more psychological. One time I was walking from PE to my ESL class, and these two kids, when they found out I was Mexican, kept calling me names like beaner and kicking my backpack from behind. Little did they know my friend Claudio was looking at them from afar and as soon as I turned the corner and left the trajectory, Claudio ran and followed them, grabbing one of them with his hand up against his face and crushing his reading glasses and told him in the worst most broken English you could hear from someone, saying, "If I ever see you do that to my friend, I'll kick your ass." I didn't know about this until the next day when they were surprisingly nice to me and I thought it was a trap or an ambush, so I kept my guard up, and when I got into class, Claudio asked me if "those guys were bothering me anymore." Thanks to Claudio my hatred towards Caucasian kids wasn't as bad, where was he when I needed someone like him in New Orleans.

Once in Amador High School, I had family I could hang around if needed, which were Jorge and Adelita Tinoco, Marco and Alicia Flores—both of their moms were my dad's sisters—and it felt good being around family. My parents were asked by Sandra (another of my dad's sisters) to go with them to Brentwood, California to an open house to help them translate. There was a new neighborhood being built next to a brand-new middle school called Bristow, and they wanted to see if they could purchase a house. When my dad asked about him and my mom, it turned out my parents qualified more than my uncles' and decided to go ahead and get a house in Brentwood.

The day I had to get a paper signed by all the school staff like my teachers, librarian, principal etc... for the school to release me was a really depressing day for me.

The last teacher to sign my paper was my math teacher, and when he asked me where was I moving to, I said Brentwood, and then he says "Brentwood? There's nothing but farmers and cows." I couldn't believe after living in Guadalajara, New Orleans, and even Pleasanton, which wasn't a big city but at least it didn't have cows, now I would be thrown to a farming community. The thought would stay in mind forever, and worse yet, when I got to Brentwood, seeing nothing but fields of corn, cherry, and strawberries made me depressed even more. Just when I was beginning to make friends from all that moving around, I had to move... again. Worst of all, I was at the puberty stage of thirteen years old, ripped away from my friends and family, in total emotional hell.

Our first home in California. Picture taken in 1996

We moved to Brentwood, California in the late fall of 1994 where, by this time, my mother would tell me at a later time my parents were promised amnesty from a lady who guaranteed they would fix their status with a residency card. "Yolanda" took $3,000.00 dollars from my parents and about twenty other families in hopes for legalization. The federal minimum wage in 1994 was $4.00 dollars an hour and three thousand was a lot of money but worth it in the long run. My parents, along with two of his sisters and their families paid the hefty amount because you do what you can to move forward. This would result in Yolanda running away with the money and never to be seen again. The reason my parents believed in this lady is she submitted paperwork signed by my parents to INS and my parents received a temporary green card for a year and what my parents didn't know is they would have a day in court to state their case as well as all of the people duped by Yolanda. We officially were deported by a federal court and ordered removed from the country immediately as of 1994.

When we moved to Brentwood I went through a depression state. I had left my friends, and by this time, I was hanging out with my cousin Jorge Tinoco who lived in Livermore, California; that's a city next to Pleasanton. Brentwood was half an hour to the north of Pleasanton and Livermore connecting the two places by Vasco Road. My parents. made it very clear they weren't going to take me every weekend to Livermore. One weekend when it rained too hard my mom didn't want to take me, I went back to my room so mad I set my alarm for 5:00 A.M. and decided I was going to leave on my bicycle and pedal my way through the storm. I was hopeful the storm would pass through by the time I would wake up because Vasco Road in those days wasn't like the nice smooth road it is today.

I left my parents a note stating if they weren't going to drive me to Livermore, I would find a way to get there by any means necessary. I went to sleep and at 5:00 A.M. sharp my alarm started to sound off and with every teenage hormone in one hand and my focus and determination on the other hand, I got changed, grabbed my bike, and started pedaling. I went through the streets of Brentwood still enraged from the night before with only one thing in mind, to get to Livermore. As I exited Brentwood, I got a flat tire before I reached the Vasco Road hills and started thinking if I should go back home or keep going. I was still pissed off enough to decide I should keep going, a little flat tire wasn't going to stop me reaching my goal.

The Vasco Road hills were a lot more dangerous back then; there was barely any space to pull over in case you got a flat tire and as you turn into a curve, they were sharper. Every time a vehicle would pass me by, my whole body would rumble, and I remember thinking that at any moment I was going to be thrown into the abyss that awaited me at the bottom of the hills. The worst part was when semi-trucks would pass right next to me and made me realize their monstrosity next to me, but I would not turn back. I was fourteen years old, and in my very naïve mind, invincible.

Peddling with a flat tire is when improvisation shines or what I thought at the time was a great idea was whenever I would get tired, I walked uphill, then, as the road shifted downhill, I would ride it down. Every time I went down, it felt I took a breather and was able to keep going. I never let my fatigue beat me. I didn't remember to bring anything to eat or a bottle of water, but my perseverance kept me focused. After five hours and about twenty miles of curvy road I reached my destination, which was Livermore. At the end of Vasco Road, there's this hill that, where they lay a road right in the middle of it and from far away it looks like the road splits the hill perfectly even in two and when you come down, you are now looking at Livermore. When I was going up walking, I couldn't wait to ride it down on my bike. As I was coming to the pinnacle of the hill when a good Samaritan in a pickup truck decided to stop and give me a lift. He dropped me off outside the apartment complex where my cousin lived, and I thanked him for his gracious decision to pick me up. My goal was met by 10:00 A.M., arriving at the front door tired, thirsty, and anxious to rest.

When I knocked on the door my cousin Adelita answered and asked me where were my parents. I told her they were home, so she automatically thought I came by bus, but when she gave me her assumption, I told her I had come in my bicycle. I saw her eyes got big and almost fell backwards and told me to use the phone and to call them immediately. When I called home, my dad answered and asked me where I was. I told my dad I was at my aunt Eva's house and then proceeded to ask me how did I get there. I answered with "I came on my bicycle." He didn't yell or get mad, but the silence between my answer and what he said next a couple of seconds later was enough for me to know he was upset. He told me they would come for me later and hung up the phone. I never knew what went on in his mind at the time of the call or what he did when he hung up. What was going through his mind when he knew I wasn't in my room asleep or home nearby. It's something I may ask him later when the time is right.

Our second home in California. Picture taken in 2005

I started to make friends in Brentwood. We lived right next to Bristow Middle School for the next eight years until 2002 when my dad got the opportunity to buy a house with more square footage. I remember I was in the garage cleaning the rims of my car when my mom told me they sold the house and we had to move within a month and quickly started looking for a house. This time it would be in Oakley, California, a town next door without the urban sprawl infesting Brentwood. By this time, I got accustomed to living in towns where there wasn't a lot of movement like the city life and actually enjoyed it.

Knowing by this time it was impossible to get a driver's license in California thanks to the politics of Pete Wilson in the '90s, I had to go get one by other means. My dad had a sister in Wisconsin where the laws towards the undocumented were more lenient and invited me over to get one. I left by plane with my community college ID and some DMV papers I acquired when I first went to see if I was able to get a driver's license in California. There was a layover at Chicago's O'Hare airport and then, arriving in Madison, Wisconsin where my aunt and cousins waited for me. I spent a month in Wisconsin as vacation buy primarily to obtain a driver's license. I noticed it was more laidback than California. I had an expired passport and a current social security card along with proof of residency my uncles provided for me, and I was able to get a driver's license. I came back to California with a driver's license happy thinking it was going to be the end of my problems.

California law states if you have an out of state license you are required to change it to a California license within thirty days or it would be as if you didn't have one. I remember about three months after I was driving, I got pulled over after I had gone to get Starbucks coffee with a friend and the cop asked me how long I had been driving and I said about three months so guess what? They took the car away, and my depression hit yet again and the reality of being undocumented made my world very real.. It's like it didn't matter that I had to go through all the trouble of getting an out-of-state license. The car was impounded for thirty days and my mom the next day went with me to the police station to talk to an officer. They took us to an interrogation room, the kind you see on TV where there is a tinted black window in the background and talked.

My mom told the officer we were undocumented and they need the car to get to work and to have mercy on the thirty day impound grace period. You can tell the officer's face filled with sympathy. He asked us to wait there and left the room, and I told my mom if that was a smart move to let them know, and I remember her telling me "either they'll give us the car back or deport us." The officer came back with a piece of paper stating we do not need to pay the thirty-dollar-a-day fine for the thirty days and we could pick it up right away. I can only imagine the frustration my mom went through at the time I guess when you're cornered it doesn't matter if it's going to end bad, you'll do whatever it takes to end the nightmare immediately.

Having an out-of-state license didn't help at all, and now I would have to hide or lie again whenever I would get stopped by the police. I still had to work and go to school, but now whenever I got pulled over, I was either on vacation or visiting. II hated lying but it becomes natural, but there was no other option at the time. a piece of paper divides a person from being legal or illegal. The only reason a person like me is illegal is the mere fact I was brought here from somewhere else, and now I have to suffer the consequences. The legal person has the right to take everything for granted while the undocumented get to enjoy living in the shadows and in fear or persecution.

My dad once told me a guy came into Home Depot where he worked and told him he didn't like illegals because all of them came and used up the welfare system and the government handouts. My dad responded with "in Mexico there is no welfare system. If you don't work you die of starvation." In other words, Mexicans don't understand the concept of the welfare system unless they are second or third generation US born.

When I first went to Wisconsin, my uncle noticed I was a good worker and invited me back the next year not as a vacation but to work at his painting company, which I accepted right away. My father didn't like the fact I was going for the whole summer and when he phoned my uncle and asked him if it was all right for me to be there for the summer my uncle responded with "I wish he'd come and stay for the whole year," to which my dad felt better, thinking I wasn't going to overstay on my upcoming "vacation."

I arrived and it was strictly "right to business." I thought I was going to be painting with some of his guys but instead he had told me he opened up a restaurant in the tourist part of Wisconsin called "Wisconsin Dells" about an hour northeast of Madison, and he wanted me to "run it" for him. On the summer of 1999, I was in charge of a small restaurant that I knew nothing of but had to get it together and learn fast. This restaurant was attached to a bar and we weren't allowed to sell liquor because the owner of that restaurant had an understanding with my uncle that he would send us the drunks so we could feed them and we would buy the liquor from him. When I say "attached" I mean if you were looking at these two places from across the street you would think it'd be the same place, but it was actually a bar and a restaurant. The only entry way separating them was a double door in the middle of the two establishments.

This restaurant was located on the corner street, and it was right in the middle of Wisconsin Dells and attracted a lot of customers for being new. This was my routine for the next month and a half: I woke up early (I'm going to guess around 6:00 A.M.) I had to get ready, then drive and pick up the two cooks (one Caucasian, one Mexican) drive an hour to the Dells and drop them off at the restaurant while I go to the bank and get change for the cash register and come back to the restaurant to get everything ready for people to show up and dine in.

After tables and chairs were where they needed to be, I had to sit people down, take their order, bring their food, ask them if they were okay or if they needed anything else, take their food away, give them the bill, take their payment, and then clean up after they were gone so the table would be ready for the next customer. At the end of the day, I had to put all the chairs on top of the tables, vacuum, take both of the cooks home, and start again in the morning. This would be my life for the next six weeks, though after four weeks, my

12

uncle decided for us to take Mondays off because the restaurant wasn't making enough revenue for it to be open on Mondays.

Our schedule was Sunday through Fridays 8:00 A.M. to 10:00 P.M. and Saturdays from 8:00 A.M. to 2:00 A.M. Mondays was slow because Mondays are always slow. Who wants to go out on Mondays? And Saturday was karaoke night at the bar next door and we had to wait until they closed so we can close and go home. Some Saturdays were really long and the two cooks didn't get along that well and another one of my jobs was to translate their arguments because the Mexican cook didn't speak English and the Caucasian cook didn't speak Spanish and when they bumped heads, I always had to be in the middle of it.

When you get thrown into a world where you literally have to learn fast, you adapt; it's human nature, even when you mess up and have to say I'm sorry on a daily basis. By the second week, I made a map and knew I had fifteen tables inside and two tables outside by the front door and had everything down because after you do it several times, it becomes repetition. I wasn't allowed to take any tips given to me because my uncle thought my cousin and I were going to fight over it, even though he was never there and when he was, he would come and try to boss me around because he thought he could.

After a while I started jacking the tips. I didn't care. My cousin didn't want to help me and my uncle didn't want to hire more help, so it felt like stealing, but it was rightfully mine, then I told my aunt, and she was okay for me to "steal my own tips." When I was there, I had it organized so well I was able to get by. I didn't even have to take breaks anymore. I didn't even have to take a lunch because whenever anybody left any of their food on the plate and I would take it to the back where the dirty dishes were, as I was placing the plate on the industrial sink, I would eat up all the food within a matter of seconds and drink whatever drink they were having and keep going. I didn't have time to take a twenty-minute lunch because there was no one to cover me. I was it.

I learned to eat leftover food from paying customers who couldn't eat their plate for whatever reason it was. So, thank you to all of you who went to the restaurant and didn't want to take your food home or else I would've really starved.

One of the Saturday nights for some reason the Caucasian cook didn't come with us, so it was just the Mexican cook and I riding in the van that I was using, which "broke down" at 2:00 A.M., and yes, it was one of those long Saturdays that we had to close late because there was karaoke night. We ended up taking a nap in the middle of the "belt line" (freeway for all you non-Wisconsonites). After so many minutes passed by and the state trooper passed by and knocked on my window, waking me up and asking me what was going on. The State trooper was nice enough to call a tow truck who charged me $80 for five gallons of unleaded gasoline (remember this was 1999). Luckily, I had the money from the cash register to pay them with and off I went and no I wasn't going to pay it with my tip money if that's what you were thinking.

The problem began when I said "yes" to all of this, but it didn't really start to affect me until the next day of when the van broke down. My cousin didn't want to let me borrow his car, even though his license was suspended and my uncle said "you have to stay near the restaurant" instead of driving back and forth, which I would've been okay if it wasn't for the place he got us literally sat on top of the bar. When you went up there, it looked like Party Central, if I was on vacation it would've been the perfect spot, but I wasn't it was a party haven for European exchange students who came over for the summer to have a good time, the whole place was disgusting. One Mexican cook and I ended up sleeping on the floor of the restaurant, which was quieter and cleaner.

One of the many things that sucked was that we didn't shower and we probably stunk up the place by the second day. By the next day, I was done with my summer; I wanted to go back home to California and luckily my dad called the restaurant to ask how I was doing and for the first time in my adult life—because I was eighteen at the time about to turn nineteen in a few months—I wanted to cry. I felt like such a pussy but working every day, not being able to relax, not being able to take a shower, not being able to take a breather throughout the day takes a toll on your psyche, and after I hung up with my dad I broke down and cried for a couple of seconds…and it was just a few seconds 'cause I had customers coming in and out and I had to keep it together.

My plane ticket was not until two more weeks, and my dad decided I should come Home sooner than later. He bought me a train ticket from a train station in downtown Chicago, Illinois to Sacramento, California. A couple of days before I was to leave, I was to talk to my uncle about my payment, and we were standing on his driveway when he hit me with it. He said waiters and waitresses in the state of Wisconsin earn approximately four dollars an hour, and he was going to pay me that. My jaw dropped and I repeated what he said just to make sure I was hearing correctly. My eyes stared at him as if he had a picture of a middle finger across his forehead flipping me off and laughing at me at the same time.

The reaction I had must've made an impression because he changed what he had previously said without me saying another word and said, "Well, I can pay you what I pay the cooks, which is $600 a week," and I responded with "okay that seems more fair," and I left it at that. I came home and my friend Martin Galindo and his brother Marco picked me up from the Sacramento train station a couple of days later.

We moved to Oakley in 2002 after living in Brentwood eight years and wasn't as a drastic change as the other times because it was fifteen minutes away from the town next door. The friends I made through those years were in driving range and even some of them helped us move. I had gone to Wisconsin when I turned twenty-one to renew my license because in the United States, even though you are an adult at eighteen years of age you are prohibited from drinking alcoholic beverages. You can be sent off to war and fight for your country, but don't expect a goodbye drink even if there's a possibility you're not going to be able to come back.

In 2003 after my dad worked for Home Depot for more than eleven years he was let go because there was a supervisor who didn't like him and was finding ways to punish him every time. He finally got fired for not putting on his seat belt while operating a forklift, and it didn't matter he was the only California Certified Nursery man in his department.

Thanks to this move made by Home Depot, he focused on getting his contractor license, and on March 22, 2004 Messina's Landscaping was founded by my dad. I joined him a couple of months later after he got too busy to do it alone, and was his righthand from their forward.

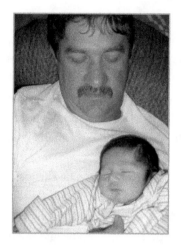

My dad, Joel Omar Messina, holding my son, Joel Alexander Messina, about a week old at my parents' house in Oakley, California. Picture taken in 2004.

In May 22, 2004, my son, Joel Alexander Messina, was born, I and named him after my father Joel and my favorite general Alexander the Great. His intelligence amazes me day by day. When he was born, I was still living with my parents and my parents helped me raise him to the point he sometimes thought my parents were his parents. I had him almost every weekend, and he became part of the family since day one. That's the year I was to meet my future wife, Maria Garcia, and when I met her, I enjoyed every minute of her company; we had a lot in common. She could be in any environment and I always had a good time with her. She was a positive person all the way through her core.

On January 31, 2006 my loan officer handed me the keys to my first home with the help of my parents about five minutes from where they lived. I knew by the time I started to pay a mortgage it was going to be nearly impossible to take a trip and asked my brother and Maria if they wanted to take one last trip to somewhere we've never been. We spent the New Year of 2005 to 2006 in New York visiting places like the Empire State Building, Time Square, Little Italy, and Chinatown.

When we came back, since I had been dating Maria for a couple of years now and had a stable job through Messina's Landscaping, I decided to pop the question on a trip we took to Las Vegas, Nevada. On April of 2006 Maria and I took a trip to Vegas and my intensions were to ask her to marry me. It was the perfect trip starting from the airport as we were checking our luggage through a computerized screen it asked me if I wanted to upgrade to first class by paying $300 dollars more. I paid for it since I've never been in first class and the forty-five-minute ride to Vegas was nice and comfortable. I had a merlot, which was free in first class, and the flight attendant saw I still had a full glass and told me to "chug it" because we were about to take off and I said, "It's a merlot?"

He said, "Come on! You never went to college!" so I chugged it in three seconds and felt very uncivilized.

They gave us more free drinks after we were in the air but overall enjoyed our flight. We stayed in the Caesars Palace and got the room with the best view; the window overlooked the strip and it was in the center of the hotel. When we went out to walk the strip, I didn't know where to propose. I saw the Eiffel tower and thought it was perfect, but when I asked about how to get to the top of the tower, the security guard told me it was closed due to high winds. We went back to Caesars Palace and dined at Bertolini's Italian restaurant and then I thought it was the perfect moment.

After we ate, I pulled out the ring and asked her to marry me. Her face filled with anxiety and excitement and she said yes. When we went back, we told our parents on separate occasions, then went forward and started to plan how we were to be married.

TOP: our civil union at the Caesar's Palace in Lake Tahoe.

BOTTOM: My maternal grandparents signing as witnesses. My brother Ruber videotaping.

In May of 2006, my maternal grandparents visited us for a month and Maria and I. decided it was the perfect time to get married while they were here, so on May 13, 2006 Maria and I exchanged vows in Lake Tahoe. Maria's family and our family were present along with my grandparents who were witnesses, signing the papers needed for our legal union.

Maria and I immediately asked about how to adjust my status and started with a legal counselor in Stockton. Maria was working at Valley Community Counseling when we got married, and through her friends was able to get us the number of a counselor who specializes in immigration. My mom went with me and I was telling the counselor a brief history of our case. Everything was fine up until he asked if there were any letters or documents sent by INS, and my mom quickly interrupted and said yes. He couldn't do anything until he saw those papers and the appointment came to a halt. We went back the next day with the letters my mom had for so many years.

On our drive back to Oakley my mom had told me the government sent us letters of deportation to my uncle's house in LA. The relationship my mom and I had was the closest of any two people. We had told each other for years a lot of things in confidence, and it surprised me she never mentioned these letters of removal until the day we headed back from the counselors today. She probably didn't want me or my brothers living in complete utter fear. She showed them to me when we got home and then went to Stockton the next day to show them to the counselor. He said he couldn't continue the process because these letters were pretty bad, and he would have to send us to a lawyer to proceed with our case.

He told us if it wasn't for those letters, within three months by paying a fine, I would've been a resident without a problem. The lawyer he recommended was from Sacramento called Sorenson and our next step was to go to her and see what she was able to do to help us.

I had envisioned our honeymoon in Spain or Italy while my case was being looked at and Maria started to focus on the wedding party, as I called it, where it would be a Catholic ceremony and then your typical reception party afterwards filled with food, drink, and dancing. I was never a religious fanatic when I was a kid. My parents raised me Catholic and went to mass but founded boring after they would talk about the same things over and over and in my mind never really seemed to impact anybody. I never grasped the concept of praying to a crucified Jew nailed to a wooden cross over two thousand years ago who never even spoke my language, it doesn't seem logical to me.

We had to ask permission to get married in a Catholic church, and when we had a meeting with the priest, Maria had asked me not to say anything stupid and to behave. I told her I wasn't going to get into any kind of verbal argument with him, but I wasn't going to lie either. I was amazed the way the priest handled the conversation and it's a touchy subject for many, but it worked out just fine. The only vivid question I remember the priest had on his mind was why get married in a Catholic Church? I answered simply because of tradition. My parents were married in the Catholic Church and Maria's parents were married in a Catholic Church and we wanted to follow the same tradition. He looked at me and without blinking, he told me he admired my honesty and gave us permission. Maria was shocked the father didn't continue to ask me anything, and I was happy with the outcome.

Our Catholic wedding picture next to the church. We got married along with all attendees including family and friends from Mexico, Canada, the United States, and Chile. Picture taken by photographer Erik Valdez.

When the time came to get married, I had invited more family than friends and a lot of people showed up including family from Jalisco, Mexico, Quebec, Canada and in the States my family from Wisconsin, LA, and all over the San Francisco Bay Area. The wedding was August 11, 2007 in Brentwood, California at the Immaculate Heart of Mary Catholic Church on the corner of Fairview and Central. The reception was in Lodi, California, near Galt where Maria's family was from at the Lodi Grape Festival Grounds.

The honeymoon had to be in Hawaii even though my original plans were to go to Europe.

I decided to invite my brother Jonathan and my cousin Wensy from Wisconsin because I wanted to do fun things like swim with the sharks and parasailing while Maria wasn't really the extreme type.

From left to right: Omar Messina, Maria Messina, Jonathan Messina, and my cousin Wensy Melendez. Picture taken on February of 2008 at the Luau in the west part of Oahu, Hawaii.

My lawyer at the time, Mrs. Sorensen, had told me she found a way to adjust my status, but I had to leave the country for a couple of months and come back legally. By this time the tensions in Mexico between President Calderon and the cartels were at full throttle and the news of the violence made me wary of the situation. In March of 2008, I joined the Oakley American Karate Academy headed by Sensei Tom Bright with his wife Jennifer Bright, who taught the little dragons that were kids from three to ten years old.

From left to right: my sensei Tom Bright, Ralston Gracie, Master Carley Gracie, and Omar Messina. Picture taken in the summer of 2010 at the Oakley American Karate Academy.

We changed lawyers because we didn't see Sorensen motivated enough and she wasn't giving us the results we were hoping for. We were referred to Julia Vera, also from Sacramento, by Maria's friend. Julia said within a year and a half, I would have my residency and told us it was an easy case. Her enthusiasm convinced us she was the right person for the job and I hired her immediately. Especially when she told us there was no reason for me to leave the country and everything could be done internally. I was already hooked in martial arts, and by this time, Ralston Gracie, the son of Master Carley Gracey of

San Francisco was teaching Brazilian Jiu-Jitsu on Wednesdays at the dojo where I went.

By 2009 my driver's license was to expire again. In Wisconsin the driver's license expires every eight years whereas in California its every four years. In one of the meetings we had with my lawyer, I let her know I had to go to Wisconsin to renew my driver's license, and when she asked how would I go, I told her the same way I've always done it, which is by plane. She highly recommended I find another means than by plane because an airport is an international gate at the federal level, and I could be pulled aside to question my status at any given time. The next fastest way to get to Wisconsin would be by train via Amtrak.

I bought my ticket a week before my birthday, and my mom and Maria dropped me off at the train station in Sacramento on a Friday morning. The pamphlet said it would take the train fifty-two hours, including thirty-two stops in seven states. Every stop was around five minutes and only one was forty-five minutes in Salt Lake City, Utah. When I arrived to Chicago on Sunday, a bus took me to Madison, Wisconsin. I had to return the same way, but this time I wouldn't have to worry about anything until the year 2016.

I came back the same way, and even though I primarily went because I had to renew my driver's license, the time I spent on the train was a very nice experience. We passed through Donner Pass, we followed the Colorado River for several hours, and I met people that like to travel by train. Dinner was included and one of the times as I went to the section of the train where you eat, in order to fill up seats, they sat me next to three black kids and my mood went from good to bad. It brought me memories of when I had to eat by them in the cafeteria and was made fun of and quickly lost my appetite. As I was lost in this mood, I noticed the kids where communicating in French. I said "parle vouz francais?" they responded with "oui." I continued "Je suis le fenetre" and started to laugh and asked me if I knew what I had told them. They said I told them "I was a window" and from there and on we had a pleasant dinner; I then realized I shouldn't have judged too quickly.

Since our wedding was so successful in the eyes of my dad's side of the family and there hadn't been a congregation of my dad's brothers and sisters since my uncle Rene's funeral (the oldest of fourteen kids) back in 1993 in Guadalajara, Jalisco. It dawned on me the idea of a family reunion with the sole purpose as to get together without celebrating nothing but the friendship we all share as a family. The Messina family spread over three countries on the North American continent. I took the job in organizing this reunion, and my wife Maria played a key role in helping me achieve it.

The Mesina Loera family from Quebec, Canada were in charge of making the invitations while I looked for a place to have it as well as to have it catered. We decided to inscribe a poem my grandmother made strictly for the reunion, and on November 27, 2009 in Marsh Creek in Clayton, California came about. All the families attending chipped in $150 each for the salon rental and food.

The main reason the date was chosen out of a lot of others was because in the United States there's a holiday called Thanksgiving and a lot of people get the time off to be with family and there is no school. It's a time to give thanks and it started back when the pilgrims where rescued by the Indians and had a feast in which turkey is the main dish. I had prepared a special gift for everybody thanks to a friend I had in Long Beach, California—Jose Hernandez. He works at an advertising company and I decided to make sixty shirts with the reunions date and location.

When everybody at the reunion was in their own world having a good time and talking with each other, I made an announcement. I went up to the microphone, lowered the music and told everybody there would be a new member of the Messina family arriving soon. Everybody started looking at their dates as if I was announcing an engagement of someone, and then I pointed to my wife Maria and everybody went to go give her a hug. She was two months pregnant with our first child, and I couldn't have been happier than at that very moment.

She had told me a couple of days before, and I told her I wanted to announce it at the reunion. While everybody was congratulating my wife, my cousin Ernie came up to me and said, "Good job; everybody congratulates the wife and not the husband." We hadn't told my parents yet, and when they heard, my mom came and hugged all three of us with teary eyes, Maria, myself, and our new addition to the family growing in Maria, who she nicknamed "bun."

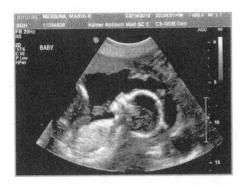

Sonogram provided by Kaiser Permanente. "Bun" was five months old. Sonogram taken in March of 2010.

The economy started to spiral downward into a fiscal abyss. It was hard to find sufficient work to keep the three full-time employees we had and we ended up with just one, Ruben Linares. The housing development took a dive and the banks didn't want to work with us, so we ended up losing my parents' house and they had to move with Maria and I until they found a house to rent. I had stopped paying my mortgage because there wasn't enough work to keep paying it and instead started to save in case the opportunity to buy another house came around. They saw the same fate happening to us and had to save up enough money to buy another house or rent before the baby came.

I wanted Maria and I to have a son because my mom had three sons, and then I had my first kid, which was a boy, and I couldn't imagine myself having a girl. I felt I wouldn't know how to raise her; besides the women in my dad's side of the family had a strong sense of character and sometimes difficult to socialize with. My mother and Maria strongly wanted a girl while my brother Jonathan and I hoped for another boy. Maria and I went to the doctor at the appointment where we would know the sex of the baby and then gave us the news: we would have a little girl. It hit me like cold water in the middle of winter, and I started to think to myself, *how will I raise a girl?*

I never grew up around them, and I was afraid I wouldn't know how. Was I going to be overprotective to the point of making her hate me? When the time is right for her to have friends or boyfriends am I going to be strong enough to guide her correctly, to let her know it doesn't matter what time of day or night it is that she can count on me to be there for her if she's ever in peril? Do I start collecting knives, guns, and hand grenades for future assholes thinking of taking advantage of my future princess? My cousin Jorge's friend told me what had happened to him and that he wanted a boy also and when his girl was born, she was the apple of his eye and his irrational thoughts and questions like I was having were normal and soon I would see the light once she was born.

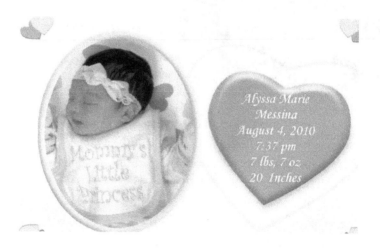

After all the baby names, we thought I preferably liked Spanish or Italian names but not from the bible. I didn't want her having two names; I have two names and I never use my first name for anything, so I didn't want the same thing happening to her. We decided "Alyssa" was the one we liked, but my wife's friends liked the name "Marie," which is Maria in Italian and I liked Alyssa because it was "Alicia" in Greek, which was my mother's name. On Wednesday August 4, Alyssa Marie Messina was born at 7:37 P.M. at the Kaiser hospital in Antioch, California after a ten-hour labor process, which was really not that bad

I didn't feel a thing, my wife did and it looked like it hurt. What helped my wife in her labor process was I used to take her to the gym I went to and walk in the pool. It's good for women to exercise when they're pregnant and makes it easier at the time of delivery, so the pool idea was perfect because when she walked, she carried the full extent of her weight and the baby's without a problem.

I had two-yard maintenance routes I kept on Wednesday and Thursdays I had to do, and when Maria started going into labor, my sister-in-law came from Galt to take Maria to the hospital while my dad came and switched trucks with me so I could go to the hospital and be with her. The first thing I told her: "DO NOT have Alyssa on a Wednesday" because it's not like I can call in to have a day off. I have a business to run so there she goes. It's like Alyssa did it to teach me a lesson. On a freakin Wednesday!

When I got to the hospital, they had Maria under a strong dose of drugs to keep her calm and pain free. They advised us when the baby is to be born not to let her out of our sight at any time for security purposes. Only one time they took her somewhere else, and by that time, my father was there to follow the nurse wherever they took her. The bath and all the necessary exams were done right there in the room with us. Before Alyssa was born, we had found the house we were going to buy, and since it was going to be under Maria's name, she had to do the signing.

I remember her signing all the documents while she was in bed with pain-killers, and I felt bad making her sign the documents under that condition, but it needed to be done by that day for our real estate agent to close escrow.

My mom tells me the story of when I was born. I was taken to get cleaned up, and when they brought me back to my mom, she said I looked different. Somehow, I had this darker complexion, the tag on my toe didn't have my dad's last name. It had my mom's maiden name and the nurses had brought my mom the wrong baby. The nurses kept saying it was me, but my mom didn't feel it was me and after a few times going back and forth, the nurses went back and brought baby me back into my mom's arms. The room Maria was in was equipped to give birth and stay a couple of nights while she recuperated.

It had a TV and a sofa where I spent the night Alyssa was born. The nurses used to call her "baby Messina." When they showered Alyssa, since I had my video camera, I was videotaping everything, and Alyssa was so mad she was screaming off the top of her lungs with her face red. When the nurse lifted

Alyssa from the bucket of water she was using, Alyssa grabbed the bucket full of water and wouldn't let go. She had a death grip on it, the nurse didn't know what to do and thought if she swung Alyssa lightly that she would let go and indeed she did but not before throwing the water all on her leg and the floor.

I knew then she was going to be strong like me and everybody in the room was surprised by the strength of this two-hour-old baby. The best part was if anybody didn't believe me, I had the video to prove it; she was a tough little cookie since the day she was born.

Maria and I saved our money in three different parts, the first part was Alyssa's college fund, the second was money we had in case we wanted to go out, and the third was our retirement money, and we would not touch it unless it was an emergency. When the economy was at its lowest starting in 2007 and finally hit rock bottom in 2009, we took advantage of the housing market and bought a house in Oakley about five minutes from where we were losing our house. We decided to put every penny we had into the down payment for the house. We couldn't get a loan through FHA because it was way out of our league, so we had to went conventional and had to put 20 percent down. It was a smaller home but still a two-story, two-bedroom, plus a nook that was satisfactory but a complete fixer-upper. The house was only in Maria's name because our lawyer Julia Vera told us for me not to be in the loan so they wouldn't take our house if something were to happen to me.

Picture taken early October after we did the roofing on the house.

On August 26, 2010 they gave us the keys to our Oakley house, and whenever my dad and I had time, we started investing the time to start fixing it. We started doing the roofing in which my father-in-law's friend helped us. We did the fence that faced the street in front of the house and the cabinets in the kitchen. The old cabinets we used as storage space in the garage. I bought new toilets and put every dime I had in it and when I depleted the money, I spent on fixing it I put the rest on the VISA credit card but didn't care because I knew whenever we had enough work to go around, I was going to pay it off. I wasn't scared at all. I was determined to make it into a home Maria wanted, and I would work on it every moment I had, painting Alyssa's room how Maria wanted it pink and purple.

From left to right: Alicia Messina, Alyssa Messina, Joel Messina and Joel Messina Sr. Picture taken at the Shirasoni Japanese Cuisine in Brentwood, California on October 15, 2010.

My mother's birthday is on October 15, and we went out to eat at this Japanese restaurant in Brentwood called Shirasoni. My parents showed up in their Honda CRV with my son, Joel; my brother showed up with his girlfriend in his '89 Honda Accord, and we came in our Lexus with Alyssa, who now was two months old. Two weeks later, when it was my birthday, I didn't really want to do anything special. There were a lot of factors like the birth of Alyssa and the fact I turned thirty, which I didn't take really well.

I kept saying I was old and it was downhill; my parents still wanted to go out and we went to Olive Garden, but when we came back, I just wanted to relax and not do anything so we stayed at my parents' house to relax, you know like old people tend to do.

My birthday landed on a Friday that year, and to my surprise my uncles from Pleasanton and Livermore came to visit, and we had a very good time. My brother Ruber gave me a forty-ounce of beer and my brother Jonathan gave me a cigar to which I responded "who's going to bring me the pot and cocaine? What do I look like?" We all had a good laugh that I remember to this day. We kept conversating, reminiscing, and hanging out until the late night came and everybody went home.

When I had my yard maintenance routes on Wednesday and Thursday, I would plan the tasks the night before on Tuesday so the next two days would go smooth. On Tuesday October 26, 2010, Maria and I would go to sleep, and I would wake up next to our munchkin who slept in her crib at the foot of our bed. A few weeks before that night while I walked and rocked my princess to sleep, I had made her a promise that nothing in this world would ever separate us and I would always be there for her, no matter what.

Picture taken on August 5, 2010 by my mom Alicia Messina a day after Alyssa was born. This is one of the ways she goes to sleep and still does to this day.

THE DEPORTATION AND REPATRIATION

This was written November 8 of 2010 at 4:36 P.M. and finished at 12:36 A.M. in Copan #87

It was Wednesday the 27th of October when Maria's cell phone wakes us up at approximately 7:00 A.M. and she answers. She doesn t understand what the person is saying and passes the phone to me in which the female voice tells me she needs to speak to Joel's brother, and while I m still waking up I ask her to repeat what she said. She tells me her name is Minerva and needs to speak to Joel's brother and when I look at the caller ID, I see she's calling from my dad's house. I knew something was wrong and immediately got into defense mode and asked the person who I don't know with a firm voice who is she and what is she doing at my parents' house.

As soon as I said "my parents' house" she started crying and she said, "I'm a friend of Ruber's and they're deporting your dad and they're taking them to San Francisco." It hit my brain like a mental slap, and I usually take a while to wake up, but with this I was alert within seconds. I gave her my thanks, looked for my uncle Pablo's cell phone number, gave it to her, and as I was hanging up the phone, I was at the window looking to see if anybody was coming for me. I started panicking and told Maria I was going to make a run for it 'cause I had a very nasty feeling they were coming this way but she told me not to leave her and Alyssa alone. I looked at the window again and saw nothing out of the ordinary and started to dial Pablo and Essie's house.

Maria started to panic and walked all around the room and left Alyssa on the bed. My baby was lying on the bed just happy go lucky. Maria began to receive text messages from my mom saying not to come out of the house, and Maria wanted to know what was going on, but my mom never responded back, and later on my mom told me they (ICE) caught her sending messages and took away her cell phone. My aunt Essie answers the phone and I start to fill her in on what's going on, and after I hung up, I tell Maria again that I'm going to make a run for it and go through the backyard and while Maria looks out the window again she tells me, "I don't think you're going anywhere" and tells me to look out the window, there were more than a few cars parked in the driveway and across the street. I ask my aunt Essie if she could come to the house just in case they take me so Maria doesn't stay by her herself, but she proposes for me to call somebody else 'cause her and Pablo would be the ideal people to go and see what's going on with my dad in San Francisco.

I go to the bathroom, and as I walk out, I call my lawyer and tell Maria to call Rubria and tell her what's going on. As Maria talks to Rubria, I leave a voicemail in my lawyer's cell phone because she never answers her calls and I tell her whatever it is she's going to do, she better hurry up. I get a call from my dad's phone, but it's not him; it's one of the agents outside the house asking me to come outside 'cause they want to talk to me. I hang up with him and remember one of our workers Ruben is on his way here, and I call him to let him know not to come at all this week, but since he doesn t answer, I hang up, and the agent calls me back again with my dad s cell phone. He tells me the same thing again and Ruben calls me back and I hang up with him again and answer Ruben's call and directly tell him not to come this week. By this time the agent starts to yell from my driveway to come out while my house is being swarmed with federal agents and unmarked cars.

The agent keeps calling me and asks why do I keep hanging up on him and tells me not to run or hide and to come out, but I tell him that I'm not running; I'm getting a bunch of calls at the same time which was semi true. I told Maria not to open the door, and if they want me, they'll have to break down the door and come for me, but she got too nervous and went downstairs to open the door. Before she went downstairs, I had told her about the key to the safe with all the important papers and $400 in cash I had inside. I put on some jeans, a shirt, some shoes along with a sweater I had on the floor because I had a pretty good feeling they were taking me to San Francisco and it was going to be cold. Maria was talking to the agents downstairs while I was changing upstairs. I took the small amount of time I had to go and look at my beautiful daughter who was lying in bed, I gave her a kiss, and even though she didn't know what was going on at two months old, I told her I had to break my promise and I didn't know when I was going to see her again. She had a baby smell that morning I still remember today and how pretty her eyes were when she looked at me and then I said "goodbye mamas," gave her a kiss on the cheek, left her on the bed, and went downstairs.

As I was walking downstairs, I started to get nervous but hid it well 'cause I didn't want Maria to notice the impotence that came over me at that moment. They asked me for an ID and went back upstairs to get my Wisconsin driver's license I had and came back down with it, put my shoes on, and went outside. The guy in charge was a small-built, baldheaded man with a connected mustache and beard. He held my deportation letters on his right hand and was telling me I had a warrant for my arrest since 1995, and everybody had a badge that said ICE (immigration Customs Enforcement) hanging from their neck.

Maria had gone up for Alyssa and when she came outside with her the agent in charge told me because I had an infant, he was going to let me stay, but I had to promise him to leave for Mexico within a week. I told him I couldn t give him such a date 'cause my lawyer had asked me not to make deals with anyone, besides I was married to an American citizen and had an existing case and told him I "needed to speak to my lawyer." Maria was outside with Alyssa both crying and all the agents started to stare at them which I then told all of them "they're American citizens" and one of them said "we only came for you nobody else." The agent told me "okay, let's go" and they put me against a black SUV parked in my driveway and started interrogating me. One of the questions they asked me was if I knew about the deportation letter and I told them that I didn't and that's why I had a lawyer.

Then they started asking me about my half sister Karina, and her whereabouts and I told them I didn t know where she was. Apparently back when my dad was trying to fix our status and got screwed over by Yolanda, my father had put in my half sister as well thinking everything was going to go well and she could live here legally and now she had a deportation warrant as well. They agents who were interrogating me were the bald guy, who Ruber told me his name was "Moser," an Asian guy next to his left, and a guy who looked Latino next to me.

I told him I didn t care if they took me back. I just felt bad for my brother's 'cause they don't know Spanish that well and they'd never been to Mexico. It looked like I struck a chord with them, but in the end, they really don't care they just come for you and take you away; it's just a job for them and most of them have to grow a thick skin.

My youngest brother, Jonathan, was living with Maria and I and tells me when they arrested him in front of my house that morning coming home from his girlfriend's house they asked if he was Jonathan Messina and he thought it was the police chasing him for a traffic ticket, and when he asked them what was it for, they told him he was going to get arrested for not showing up to court in 1994. My brother responded with "I was three years old and unable to drive myself to court" to which the agent stared at him and then responded with "well, your parents put you in this position get in the car!" they hand-cuffed him and put him in a jeep. When they were handcuffing me, I was still thinking of were my parents could be and then when they opened the door to the SUV, there they were in the vehicle the whole time with my brother Ruber also handcuffed like criminals.

My mom was sitting in the back alongside my dad, and Ruber was sitting in the seats that were closer to the door and a metal screen separated them from where the driver and the passenger seat would be. When I came in to the van I asked where was my other brother Jonathan 'cause I hadn't seen him in two days. He has this thing where he takes off with his girlfriend or friends and I don't see him. My mom told me they had him in another car and we requested for him to be with us.

The bald guy told the other agent to bring him here and when he told him he wouldn't fit we told the bald guy we would make room for him and to his response to the other agent was "bring him here; I've fit about ten wetbacks in here at one point." When that was going on, Maria came near and asked if she could bring us water, and I told her to bring me a banana 'cause I hadn t eaten anything. When she came back, I told her to tell Julia our lawyer to let her know what's going on. The bald guy told us to take off our shoelaces and if we had any jewelry to take it off too.

We took off our shoelaces and stuck them in Jonathan's backpack that was in the trunk along with my dad's and Ruber's. My dad and Ruber had a chance to make a backpack when they picked them up, and Jonathan had his backpack he takes to his girlfriend s house when he goes over. They closed the doors to the SUV, turned it on, and we left Oakley. We stopped at a Starbucks that was on Lonetree Way in Antioch 'cause they wanted their coffee before they took us to San Francisco. We were in the SUV thinking about all the possible outcomes this incident could take us whether I would stay and they didn't get to stay or all of us stay or all of us go. We took highway 4 West bound towards Martinez and knew we were destined to be in San Francisco.

We were passing Concord when my dad wanted to go pee really bad and told the driver who was the Asian guy if we could stop somewhere or else we were going to pee in the SUV, so he radioed all the other agents following us and we stopped at a gas station off of North Main St. in the city of Walnut Creek, which was about twenty minutes or so from where we live. We then began to speculate the water bottles Maria had given us were a bad idea 'cause we were going to be going to the bathroom every half an hour, so we stopped drinking them altogether.

When we got there, we went to the bathroom one by one. My dad went first, and when they asked us if we wanted to go, which by that time we all had to, so the next person would wait outside the SUV, and then when the next person would finish the next would wait outside and that's how our bathroom trip went, very systematically, they were watching us like if we were going to make a run for it or something. We took off and our driver had the AC full blast and we asked him to turn it down because we were getting cold and felt like we were going to have to pee again.

We began our talks about planning what would happen, and my dad was telling me he put in his sock some money he had when we sold our Ford Expedition a couple of weeks before. One of the talks we specifically had was if we were to be separated when we get to Tijuana we should look for a Burger King or McDonald's some type of fast food in alphabetical order and just in case we didn't find one we should get a taxicab and get dropped off at the Tijuana International Airport and go to the first airline in alphabetical order and wait for all of us to get there. We started to tell jokes and make the best of the situation 'cause our self-esteem was very low. We crossed the Bay Bridge and I told everybody to enjoy the view of the bay 'cause there's a chance we wouldn't be able to see any of it for a really long time. We crossed Yerba Buena Island and entered the city of San Francisco via highway 80 westbound and exited on Harrison St. towards the skyscraper section of the city. They took us to a building where it didn't look like a detention center 'cause it didn't have any signs posted anywhere, or at least from where we entered didn't look like much.

Picture of the bay bridge connecting Oakland with San Francisco. Picture taken in the summer of 2013

The SUV passed the entrance where we were going to park in reverse, but before they closed the garage door, I was able to see the street we were on, which was Jackson and the numbers on the building in front of us, which read "350" just in case I needed it later. They took us down from the SUV and waited until they handed us our backpacks, and in single file they took us up about five steps into the building and to the left was an elevator that took us to the sixth floor. The elevator itself was designed to have prisoners where two thirds of the elevator was for prisoners and the other third was for the agents and also it had a padlock.

They took us out of the elevator single file and they took my mom somewhere else, they had us against the wall while they took our information. Ruber and I were laughing and making jokes and one of the agents who looked Latino came over and told Ruber in a loud voice to shut up or else he was going to press felony charges on him. The fire alarm started going off in the whole building, and I was thinking it was routine but. The agents there didn't seem to know what to do 'cause it looked like it had never happened before. After they took our picture, they took off the hand-cuffs and put us in a cell where if it was really an emergency or the building was on fire, they wouldn't have cared if we were in there. The cell was about 10 feet by 30 feet, and we've never been in a more disgusting room in our lives. The cell was vandalized in every wall you'd see, and it smelled like a sewer. They had two stainless steel L-shaped benches and on the opposite side of the room were two stainless steel toilets separated by two small dividers without any privacy. When we got there, there was already about fifteen detainees and as time passed by, there was more and more until it got to about twenty-five of us.

Our lawyer Julia Vera had warned us before not to say anything to anyone if we were to be put in one of these cells 'cause sometimes federal agents will slip in an undercover agent to ask us questions that could harm us in a court of law and to our luck there were two or three individuals asking everybody all sorts of nonsense questions. We tried warning Ruber and Jonathan about it 'cause they're more prone to get suckered into that than my dad or myself first there was a guy asking where we were from and where we were going, but there was this other guy, kind of small built wearing sandals and sweat pants asking and asking until my dad started to get mad and asked him in a loud voice "are you our lawyer!" to his response was "no sorry if I offended you" and walked away.

While that was going on, I was figuring out how I was going to knock this guy to the ground if he tried something. But since we re all in the same situation there was an abundant amount of respect in the air. Since most of the people in there had either already gone through it or didn t have any family, they were making jokes and taking it lightly. Within several minutes, they called my dad first, then Jonathan and me together. They took us to another room which was on the other side of where they had us first, and it was a long room filled with federal agents and about ten computers or so, and next to those computers there was a long table filled with backpacks and personal belongings being searched, and on the wall there was a Homeland Security seal.

Detention Center building in San Francisco where hundreds of undocumented immigrants are processed. Picture taken in the summer of 2013.

When we entered the room, we started to panic 'cause we didn't see our dad, but the agent told us he was called into the visiting area and we felt better. They started processing Jonathan meanwhile I made a phone call and had to sign a paper saying I made that phone call. They took a digital picture through a webcam and took his fingerprints digitally to store them in the computer and find out if he had any previous charges and then made him sign a form saying that was his information. When they were done with him, we traded places. While he talked to his girlfriend, Rosy, I got processed.

When Jonathan and I were being processed, we started talking about what happened that morning and when the Asian guy processing us overheard, he told us when they picked up my parents and Ruber at their house, somebody called the cops on them and this is what happened. when federal agents arrived at my parents' house my brother Ruber through his computer texted my good friend Noah Lake who called Oakley Police and when they showed up, they saw a lot of activity at my parents' court for being six in the morning and not knowing they were federal agents the cops asked what they were doing there and one of the ICE agents tried to show his badge by putting his hand inside the jacket, and the cops drew their weapons at all of them and to move very slowly. Once the agents showed their government IDs the police holstered their weapons but stayed and made sure my parents weren't mistreated. The agent processing my brother and I told us "even though we work with guns we don't like getting them pointed at us. They called Ruber's name and sat him down on the desk behind us to start processing him.

None of us had eaten anything, and it was noon already, and while I was thinking when the hell was I going to eat something, a guy walks in with a little stainless steel cart that had sandwiches and my mouth started to get watery. In the plastic bag where the sandwich was you'd find a three-layered sandwich with two slices of ham a packet of mustard and a vanilla cookie and they gave you a bottle of water. The minute Jonathan and I were done being processed they told us to get up grab a sandwich with a bottled water and they took us down the hall, which in about fifteen steps, the hall continued to the left and to the right were more cells and they put us in one similar to the first one but smaller and with more people.

Within fifteen to twenty minutes, they called my name, and when I came out of the room, they put me in a small visiting room who already had a guy in there talking to someone. The room had a security camera on the top left corner, a phone which was the communicating tool between you and your visitor, a plexiglass window that divided you with your visitor, and two chairs. On the visitor's side, it had about the same dimensions which would total the room to about five feet wide by fifteen feet long and a padlock for the agents to let you in and out of the room.

As I was finishing my sandwich, my uncle Pablo and aunt Essie came in along with three of Ruber's friends Jared, Jonathan, and Valerie. I talked to my uncle Pablo first, and he was telling me he talked to my mom and dad and not to worry about anything and to tell my lawyer if she's going to start doing her job 'cause if she isn't, we need to get somebody else ASAP. My aunt Essie got on the phone and started telling me if there are any errands that need to be done and gave me my case number, which was A70 086 006. I had to memorize it in ten seconds just in case I needed it.

When I was done with my aunt Essie, Jared picked up the phone and started to tell me if I needed anything to let him know, so I gave him Maria's number so he could either swing by my house or help with anything and also to go to my parents' house 'cause it's going to be vacant for a while. I've never had the pleasure of talking to Ruber's friend Jonathan, but the few times I said hello at my parents' house, he is one of the coolest people I've ever met just by saying hello and the only thing I could tell him since I didn't know him that well was to thank him for him being there and for his support.

They were about to leave when another of my brother Ruber's friend Valerie took the phone and she did all the talking 'cause I was so choked up I was going to burst into tears if I said something, and the reason I felt like that was when she was talking she had tears in her eyes and was telling me we have the full support of her and her family and if there's anything they can do to help to let them know and all I could do is thank her with a knot in my throat. Valerie left the room and I got up and walked towards the door but remembered it can't be opened without a key from the outside so I sat there with a million things going through my mind.

Once I was there alone tears started to roll down my cheeks and the sudden impotence and low self-esteem I'd been having on and off throughout the day really took effect on me as I felt like a caged animal. The door of the visiting room had a small rectangular window that you could see a little bit of the hallway and in less than five minutes, I saw Ruber pass from right to left into the room Jonathan was in and another five minutes passed and I saw my mom pass from right to left both escorted by federal agents. Another five minutes passed, and an agent came to the door and asked if I was done and took me out and into the room where I was originally in with Jonathan. I went in and there were even more people in there, like thirty and my dad and Jonathan were there, but not Ruber.

My dad told me that they called him probably to the visiting room. My dad told me the lawyer was maybe in the building, but I told him earlier when I talked to Maria, the lawyer told her that her business was in the courtroom and not to deal with ICE. My dad said he didn't want to take the backpack with him and had my uncle Pablo sign for it so he could take it with him instead. As we were chatting for about ten more minutes or so, they called me back again to the visiting room, and this time Maria entered with my princess Alyssa who illuminated my devastated self-esteem and gave me a reason to lift up my spirit, she was so beautiful with her bib and her little toes and hands looking at me behind this glass wall.

Maria and I were talking about the current situation and I could hear Alyssa making her baby noises, and I couldn't take my eyes off of her. I'd have to tell Maria to keep talking 'cause she thought I wasn't paying attention I was just focused more on Alyssa and getting another glance at her, which would turn out to be my last one. She looked so beautiful and through the plexiglass, I made her smile and to this day I still remember the funny little scream of joy she made with her pink outfit and her bib; she looked so cute. Maria cleared all doubt in my mind about my lawyer Julia being in the building she said the worst case scenario was for everybody to stay put until Friday, or maybe there's a chance today within three hours or so, and though that was good news, the idea of us spending the night in that hellhole was upsetting, but then I thought *at least that's better than nothing.* This time I stayed in the visiting room until they came for me and after a while Alyssa started to get irritated because, this girl, if she's awake, you need to be walking up and down with her like she's taking a tour or else she isn't happy. Maria was asking me if it was a good idea for her to breastfeed Alyssa right there, but I didn't feel comfortable 'cause it wasn't that private.

There was a guy next to us talking to what appeared to be his wife, so she stood up and went to the door so my aunt Rubria could take her and we continued with our conversation. She asked me if I had time to chat more, and I told her about earlier when I was talking to my uncle Pablo and aunt Essie that when we were done, I was waiting for about fifteen minutes for them to open the door, so this time I was going to wait until they took me out. I wanted to talk about the ifs and the buts about me not being there and how she needed to take care of some things, but Maria wouldn't have it. She said to think positive and everything was going to work out, so we left it at that.

An agent passed by, knocked on the door, and said we had two minutes so we began to say our goodbyes and I told her I may be able to call collect and I was going to try and call her later tonight, and if not, I ll try calling her tomorrow as soon as I could 'cause there was phones in the cells we were at and there was a possibility they might work. They took me and they guy next to me out of the visiting room and into the cell that was to the right, which wasn't the cell I was originally in with my family, and when I told the agent, he said they're all the same thing and told us to get in and locked the door behind us.

I was in a similar room but only with seven people and decided to go take a piss in this one 'cause if you were to take a piss in the last one you might lose your seat. As I was walking to take a seat some guy asked another guy if I was Mexican and one of the guys said he's probably from Mexico City to my response was "hell no Guadalajara." I started to think about what would happen if I got separated and get to Tijuana by myself and our plan about the fast food restaurants and the airport, but then Maria had told me earlier Julia was on the prowl and taking care of business so I kept calm and sat down. Two agents came and took us all out and put us back in the cell where my family was and it was already packed.

I told the agent "You guys are really cramming the cells," and he said it was only temporary so they don't have to go cell to cell and look for people, and they shoved us in there with the forty or so guys and felt like sardines. At first there were a couple of guys lying down and another one using the trash can as a seat, but now nobody could do anything because there were so many of us in there. I started to tell my dad what Maria had told me about the lawyer being there and started to feel a little bit better. I don't think an hour passed when they started to call out names and we were one of those on their list, so we began to walk outside the door, and they told us to face the wall of the hallway while they finish roll call.

They took about twenty of us, single file, to the room where they had the computers and began to search us thoroughly with latex gloves. It was a surreal moment yet an eerie feeling at the same time when we heard the shackles and chains hitting the floor as they began to put them on all of us I turned to Ruber and said, "Do you remember robbing a bank before we got here?" When Jonathan asked an agent "why so many chains?" they told him it was because they were going to put us in an airplane, and they didn t want us to make a run for it. This time not only did they put handcuffs on us, but they wrapped a chain around our hips and tied the handcuffs to the chains and then chained up our feet together, we now had feet cuffs—if that's even a word—like we were high-risk felons.

Then I remembered my dad had the money hidden in the sock and I whispered to him it was a bad idea because they were searching deep this time. Several hours passed without knowing anything about my mom, and I asked if they were going to do the same to the women, in detention centers just like prisons and jails they have the women separated from the men They took us to the room they had us in when we first came in, but they told my dad to stay put, and I didn t know anything about him for about five minutes or so. He came in and I asked him if they had stopped him because of the money and he said yes, but he told them it was his money and they let him go. They started to call out our names again and this time they called my dad and I at the same time and they took us to the hallway where we first got our picture taken and we had to put our thumbprint on a piece of paper and sign our voluntary deportation.

My dad turns to me, and I tell the agent my lawyer told me not to sign anything, and I needed to speak to her. He said there are no calls after 3:00 P.M. and it didn t matter if I wasn't going to sign the paper, they were going to take me to Mexico anyhow. The agent grabbed my hand by force to put the thumbprint on it and signed it himself on where my signature was supposed to be and wrote "refuse to sign" and did the same thing to my dad. He explained we can no longer come into the country for the next ten years, and if we do, we are susceptible to the twenty-year ban and up to three years in prison and put us back in the room with a paper explaining the ten-year ban.

We were going back to the room slowly 'cause of the chains on our feet when I hear Ruber and Jonathan's name being called out and as we cross paths, I tell them not to sign anything and waited for them in the back corner of the room. I started to think what the agent had said about we were going to be in Mexico tonight no matter what and started to get nervous 'cause neither Maria nor the lawyer knew what was going on and there were some friends and family who were going to come visit us the next day. It must've been around forty minutes or so when they were finished with everybody giving them their deportation letters, they took us out single file through the elevator and outside into one of two buses that were ready to go to the airport. The bus looked like it could take about 150 people and a separated small space of about four towards the front and then the driver. The day had turned gray and cold, and I was sitting right next to my dad while my brothers sat next to each other in front of us.

My dad and I pondered on where my mom could be and looked out the window to see more and more people come out in chains but my mom was nowhere to be found and then she came out and we thought they were taking her to the bus in front of ours but to our surprise they put her in the same bus as us. As she walked into the small cell in the bus, some guys started to yell "the women are here!" my dad stood up so my mom could see him and some guy said "that's his wife." Then the agent told the guys in the front row to get up and go towards the back and had us sit right next to mother.

We went back to talking about what was going on because our destiny looked like we could be in Mexico by that same night. At first I thought the bus was taking us to the San Francisco International Airport but then saw that the bus got on highway 80 east through the Bay Bridge on the bottom side of the bridge heading away from San Francisco. It narrowed down to either Sacramento or Oakland, which I was hoping they were taking us to a detention center in Sacramento 'cause it's where our lawyer is based out of and she could then do her job more effective I presumed.

We took a right turn onto highway 880 South that connects Oakland with San Jose and then was real sure when it took the Hostetter exit 'cause it's where the Oakland International Airport was. The bus took a left turn way before the main entrance of the airport where all the airlines where to a private gate guarded taking us directly to the hangar where the plane stood on standby, no gates, no TSA, straight onto the tarmac. They took out all the men first and all the women at the end and told my dad we were going to be together as a family. There were about four male agents searching us again and one female agent searching the women. Still handcuffed from head to toe they put us into the plane through a stairway that opened in the back of the plane. The plane could fit about 200 or so prisoners and it had a walkway in the middle with two chairs on the left-hand side and three on the right.

When we entered the plane, there was a guy sitting us down and when I saw that they were going to separate us I told him they promised us we were going to be together, and he told the guy who was at the window seat to get up and go into the next row of seats and sat my dad next to me and a guy who had been deported twelve times next to him then Ruber and Jonathan sat together across the aisle. We saw everybody come in and at the end the women came in and when we saw my mom walk by they told her to keep going and my dad said that she was his wife and the guy told him she had to go to the front because she couldn't be mixed with the guys and my dad told him they promised to keep us together and he said he understood but explained some of them are not that nice and it was for her own protection to be in the front.

We could kind of see where she was sitting and in the end, I guess it was better this way, and we waited for the plane to take off. I hadn't flown in about two years due to the fact the lawyer had advised me not to since I had the deportation warrant against me and Ruber said he hadn't flown since the first time we went to Vegas thirteen years ago. During the flight we were given another sandwich similar to the one at the processing center to which my dad and I decided to save a piece of bread in case we got hungry later. We weren't sure where they were taking us. m My dad was talking to the guy next to him and he was saying they were probably going to take us to Yuma, Arizona while the agents on the plane were drinking coffee and sweet bread in front of us and you could see everybody's eyes just glared at the sight and the smell.

An agent passed by asking everybody who wanted to go to the bathroom and whoever did was guided to the bathrooms located in the back where another agent stood guarding the bathrooms with the doors open and when you were finished you couldn t wash your hands you had to walk back and a female agent would squirt petroleum jelly in your hands and she gave you a couple of napkins to wipe them off.

A guy walked by with the trash bag asking how long were we going to save the piece of bread and my dad s response was "a couple of hours," and then he said "you have twenty minutes" not knowing the flight was only about forty minutes long and within five minutes he passed again and we had to throw it away. The plane began to descend and slow down. I knew we were still in the States but couldn't pinpoint our exact location. We started to look around as the plane touched ground and was going through the runway, and as it was stopping, we saw a sign reading "Bakersfield Airport."

Ten minutes passed and another bus similar to the one that took us to the airport arrived with more people and began loading them up into the plane completely filling it up. We couldn't take off because there was a guy with respiratory problems and had to be attended to in front of the plane by where my mom was. This time we were only in the air for about twenty minutes, if that, and when we landed, we were in San Diego, California, and this time they took everybody out of the plane where there were buses and white vans waiting for us in the hangar. They unloaded everybody, starting with the men in the back of the plane first and put us up against the bus to take us off the handcuffs and chains.

They would take them off and then, with our hands on our heads, load us up in the bus where I took a chance and asked the agent, who was African

American, to let me use the phone 'cause I was married to an American citizen. He heard wrong and thought I said I was an American citizen, but he let me explain myself better and realized I only wanted a phone call. He said I could make it once they dropped us off in Mexico. My dad began to ask if my mom was going to be with us and they agent responded that they couldn't let her cross tonight because she's a woman, so they were going to drop us off tonight and keep her until the morning and drop her off then.

My dad demanded my mom be with him because they promised him she was going to be by his side to where they kept responding the same thing. As they were taking us into the bus, they grabbed my dad and took him somewhere else while we were inside the bus and my mom was still in the plane... . The worst-case scenario had just happened—they have separated us. All of a sudden, I started to think fast about our plan and to find a fastfood place in alphabetical order and as I planned all the possible scenarios in my head

An agent came into the bus and asked "who were the ones that were part of the family?" All three of us responded in unison and the agent said, "There's three of you? Are you kidding me?" and told us to get off and escorted us to where my dad was sitting in a white van by himself. The white van seated about eight people in the back and there was a small partition that seated four between the back where we were and the driver's seat—a perfect portable cage.

A couple of agents came to the van to ask us who else was with us and we told them my mom was the only one left and they explained they were going to let us out first before everybody in the bus and were going to let us pick up our stuff and be on our way. My dad took out the stack of money he had hidden in his socks and gave us some just in case he lost it or it was taken from him. He gave us $300 each, and Ruber put it in his pocket while Jonathan and I put it in our socks too.

My mom arrived, and they put her in the small cage and took my dad outside from where we were and stuck him in with my mom. After they unloaded everybody off the plane and into the bus, we took off on highway 5 southbound headed for the Mexican border to where the guy driving the van started to drive like a maniac and once we got on the freeway he must've been doing about 90 miles an hour, passing every single car in its path, we got so freaked out that we had to put on our seat belts.

We were more tranquil yet the shock of it all still hit us again and again like waves from a vibrant beach. I started to feel that impotent feeling again and couldn t believe what was happening I wanted to wake up, but I couldn t and I could tell the same thing was happening to all of us in there when I saw tears on Jonathan's face and Ruber's look of uncertainty. We were taken from our daily routines, our normal lives in California and were going to be thrown into a foreign land starting from zero. I remember I always tried not to get into trouble even when trouble was imminent, even when trouble was appealing as a teenager and jail time could follow, I looked away and all for what? I was in a portable cage with nothing but the clothes I had on about to be thrown like an object without a chance to explain myself in a court about to be thrown into the unknown realms of a border town plagued with violence. I could endure anything thrown at me except not being able to hold my princess Alyssa whom I had so many kisses to give her and my son Joly whom every weekend could be seen at my parents' house enjoying life to the fullest.

There was a series of feelings following my nostalgic depression; I started to feel anger in the way everything was handled, all my life I followed everything by the book. The law states if I get a lawyer I could bring my case and this could be avoided. Our lawyer painted a pretty picture when it came to my case; what happened? Why are we headed to Tijuana with nothing? Without a change to live our normal lives again? Without a fucking dime? I got angry at those pieces of shit from ICE who came early in the morning and took us half-asleep from our homes without any warning and like animals enslaved us without rights, it was all in the past now.

We arrived at the San Ysidro checkpoint in a private gated area where there was a black metal fence higher than the buses and wondered if that was the border. We stayed put in the van for about fifteen minutes while they took out our belongings from the bus and let us off. We looked for Jonathan and Ruber's bag with a small-claims note they had given us at the beginning, and when we found them we walked into the black metal fence, which had a gate in the corner and as it opened, a Mexican Federal Immigrations agent with a notepad waited for us. He asked us three questions 1) our full name 2) our age and 3) if we had kids in the United States and how many to which we all responded accordingly, and then he told us to form a line at a small building right next to him.

We had entered Mexico through San Ysidro into Tijuana but were in a confined section of the border where in a small building that read "The Institute of Immigration and Repatriation of these United Mexican States." In this particular building we were in line to get a credential that was going to let us take a bus or a plane to anywhere in Mexico. While we were looking for our shoelaces in Jonathan's backpack, I called Maria with Jonathan's cell phone to tell her what was happening and luckily the cellular still had signal. When she answered, she sounded like I had woken her up and saw it was close to midnight.

I told Maria to hurry up and get a pen and paper 'cause I didn't have much time with both signal and battery. First I told her to call Julia and tell her we got dropped off in Tijuana and second to go into my Facebook and contact a lady named Ana Maria which was our cousin Toto's and my aunt Rubria's friend from high school and she lived in Tijuana and even though I had only met her for a week in the social network she gave me a good vibe. I told her I was going to call her back in an hour while she gathers information and we go through the repatriation process.

When our number was up, an officer took our information and we stepped into the office to get our picture taken alongside our credential. When my mom stepped in the one-story building, we saw through the window she was taking long and what had happened is the webcam from the computer stopped functioning and we weren't able to have a picture on our ID. After the picture fiasco we had the option to step on the side of the building where another office presided so we could sign for a microwavable cup of noodles and a free two-minute phone call that we waived because our cell phone still worked. When I called Maria back, luckily she was connected with Ana Maria through Facebook and was chatting with her online and when she explained everything to her she gave Maria a bunch of numbers to call her from but I didn t know how to dial them so I told her to call me instead.

Maria didn't want me leaving Tijuana just in case the lawyer had a plan B and needed me there so I told her to let me know as soon as possible 'cause we didn't want to be there much longer. Ana said she would pick us up but within several minutes, but we started to feel unsettled and walked away from the repatriation center into Tijuana. As we were walking towards another metal gate that spun as you walk through it, we saw an abundant amount of soldiers with automatic weapons holstered dressed in camouflaged beige army suits who made me feel both safe and aware we were in the part of the world I only saw news on TV about the drug wars along the border. We walked past the metal gate and to the right-hand side saw a McDonald's behind a building blocking it s view, the lights were turned off probably 'cause it was close to midnight.

There were about ten to fifteen taxi drivers and about twenty taxi cabs in the back waiting for people wanting a ride. It looked like you were walking in the mean streets of LA and my dad told the guy to take us to the cheapest hotel closest to the airport and the reason for that is my dad was itching to leave to Guadajalara. It was five of us in a little yellow Nissan Sentra and my dad jokingly asked the cab driver if we had to put on our seat belts to which the cab driver responded "no don t worry about it," and we all looked at each other like we wanted to say "this is Mexico."

By the time we hit the first turn, I had lost the signal, the phone read service unavailable and couldn't get in touch with Maria anymore and less with Ana who probably was on her way by now. We got to the Hotel Principado near the airport and after my dad paid the room, which was $900 pesos or $79 dollars, Ana called and said she was by the McDonald's near the border waiting for us. I apologized and told her since we already had paid for a room and we didn't want to inconvenience her and we were going to be there the night and if she could come for us the next day before 12:00 P.M. because that was check-out time.

She insisted it wasn't an inconvenience and we could stay there for a night or two and to please consider her offer and I would've taken it, but we were already settled in the room and we left it at that; I turned off the cell phone because the battery was depleting. We stepped into room #209 and it smelled horrible like if someone had gone to the bathroom in the room instead of the bathroom and my dad went downstairs to ask if they had another room, but it was the only one.

The hotel didn't look that bad from the front; the rooms were pretty good in size with two beds in which my parents slept in one, Jony and I on the other and Ruber on the floor. I put the alarm for 7:30 A.M. 'cause they told us that's about the time they start serving breakfast but like around 5:00 A.M. we all couldn't sleep anymore. My dad, Ruber and I went to the store while Jonathan and my mom stayed in the room. We went walking to the corner store and bought some waters, a milk for me, some toothbrushes, and luckily they let us pay with dollars.

My dad had forgotten something my mom asked him to buy and went back to the store alone while Ruber and I headed to the room. We waited until 7:00 A.M. to go eat breakfast and when we got to the hotel's diner there was only one or two things on the menu, and we all had the same thing, which was potato with eggs in red sauce, beans, and tortillas, which tasted like they bought them at Walmart or something and a choice between orange juice or bottled water. We went back to the room, and I was the only one who hadn't shower so I jumped in while everybody else watched TV and rested.

Ana called me later and told me she was going to take her kids to school, and since she was self-employed she was going to clear her appointments for today and come over before noon. After some time passed, my aunt Mona called from Guadalajara and wanted to know if we were all right and not to trust anybody there and then spoke to my dad. After my dad hung up with my aunt, we couldn't put our finger on how she would've known we were there.

But after analyzing the situation, we made the connection: Ana emailed Toto and Toto got in contact with my aunt Mona and aunt Mona called us. After my aunt Mona called we started getting calls from Pablo and Rubria. Rubria told me to ask Ana an "is it really Ana" question: "What was her brother's nickname in high school?" The answer was "chicano." Ana called me around 10:30 A.M. saying she's almost done and tells me my sister called me from the other side wanting information about our whereabouts, and when I asked who it was, she said she didn t want to say her name, and after she gave her the information, she hung up not knowing who it was.

I told Ana I didn t have a sister on the other side and to call me before she gets here 'cause we may not be in the hotel anymore, so I hung up, told my dad what was going on, and rushed out of the room as soon as possible because we didn't know what kind of person or people knew our current location. We stayed in the lobby where we felt more secure and sat down on some couches they had, the phone rang in the front desk and I picked it up where we were seated because there was a phone next to a lamp. It was my aunt Sandra wanting to talk to my dad and then we figured out she was the one who called Ana and she said it was Omar's sister that meant my dad s sister not me. There was a guy outside the lobby painting the front of the building and some stray dogs walking around the streets like nothing, then my dad got hungry and decided to go with my mom across the street to get some tacos from the corner while Ruber and Jonathan talked on the couches inside the lobby.

I looked to where my parents had gone and didn t see them, so I looked over at the Pemex gas station and nothing, so I started to walk towards the street and I saw them on the left-hand side; then all of a sudden you could hear the sirens of cops coming from far away and within minutes a motorcycle cop was passing cars like they were parked and a cop truck in the back doing the same thing only with an automatic rifle sticking out of the back window, it was jaw breaking, so much that there was a lady walking by with her two daughters and stepped back to where I was and said "I don t like what I just saw, to which I agreed."

Ana called me back saying she was at the airport asking for directions on how to get here and then she said "hold on cabron!" to which I responded "Okay," and she started laughing saying she was telling that to the carbon (which is a cuss word in Spanish) behind honking at her and after that little incident I started to calm down because I was nervous to meet her. As soon as she got out of the car, I asked her what did they call her brother in high school and she didn't remember, but by that time, I didn't care because she greeted us like we were old friends.

She came with a friend in a small car and since it was five of us, we got a taxi to fit everybody and my parents, Ruber ended up going in the taxi while Jonathan and I rode with her and her friend.

As we were driving through Tijuana. I realized you had to be half psychic and half awesome to drive there; people were turning corners and changing lanes without signaling and you could hear the honking of the automobiles everywhere. It looked like chaos compared to what we were used to and Ana must've cussed at least ten times at anybody cutting us off and vice versa before we got to her house. I've never seen so many roundabouts and Aztec statues before and then on the horizon you see a gigantic Mexican flag that waves as the coastal air hits it from one side, it waves as if it was waving in slow motion.

We dropped off her friend and then went to her house and to tell you the truth I did not know how she got there because there were no street signs of any kind or at least I didn t see them. So, if you're a mailperson in Tijuana you have my full respect. Where she lived made the ghetto streets of LA look like the Garden of Eden and she was telling us the houses there were approximately $120,000.00 dollars to which I thought not even if I had $10,000.00 dollars I would live there. She made us feel like home and our paranoid state began to disappear.

I called Maria with the little battery life I had left in the cell phone and gave her the information of our location so she could spread the word that we were all right and I would give her a day to do whatever the lawyer was going to do, and then we were going to look for plane tickets to Guadalajara. We talked for a little bit on her dining table while Ruber used the internet and Jonathan played with Ana's ten-year-old kid on his Playstation 3. We went to buy some essentials we needed. We had the same clothes on for two days now but first we stopped at a gas station and we offered to pay for her gas. We went to a couple of stores, the first one to buy groceries and some underwear. As we walked to the second one, we stopped at a stand because I needed a phone charger but didn't have change. When we entered the second store, they also didn't have change so we went to change dollars to pesos but didn't want to go back to the store due to the fact that we were starving so we headed to buy some grilled chicken.

Picture of the old border and new border

As we went back on the freeway, I looked at the rocky hills next to us and noticed an old rusty fence and I jokingly said "hey, that looks like the Mexican border" to which Ana responded "it is." It was impressive to see the border up close, the old rusty fence would go into the water for another half a mile and farther back about 200 feet into the United States was a newer one more erect and tall fence and you could tell it had a more highly modernized security system that you could see as you went near it.

We got home and I wanted to change everything, but when I put on the underwear, they felt like bicycle shorts; my crotch couldn t breathe properly, and the white shirts were like for an eight-year-old, so I couldn't put them on. We received calls during the day from our uncles and none of them wanted us to stay in Tijuana a single day more, so my dad wanted me to find out airplane tickets to Guadalajara via internet. I gave him a number to call and they told him he could buy them at some place nearby before 8:30 P.M. and as soon as they found out where, my parents and Ana went to go buy them. In the meanwhile, Maria called me and I told her she had up until 10:00 A.M. to do something because we were most likely going to be on our way to Guadalajara. She told me the lawyer wasn't coming and if she did anything she was going to give me a call so I told her "in that case she can call me in Guadalajara."

While my parents and Ana were out buying the tickets Mario, Ana's husband, got home and we talked around the dining table. When they got home, my dad told me he couldn't buy them but to go to the airport anyways because my aunt Essie was going to buy them with my mom's credit card online. Ana ended up giving us her kids' room, which had two beds and the kids slept in Ana's room and Ana slept in the living room. Even though we slept real good in that room only this time Jonathan was on the floor and Ruber and I on one of the beds, at about 4:30 A.M., all of us lost our sleep and more when my parents were having a conversation in whisper mode.

We all got up and started getting ready and my dad wanted to make some noise outside the room to wake them up but I suggested on going and waking them up instead of torturing them slowly with our whispers. We finished in getting our stuff together while my dad and Mario went to look for a taxi; then Jonathan tells us he can't find his wallet that had the $300 dollars my dad had given him along with his Repatriation ID.

My dad came with the taxi, but we couldn't find Jonathan's wallet anywhere. We said our goodbyes and headed for the airport in a cab. We were driving through the streets of Tijuana and there was an instant of about two to three seconds were we panicked because the driver was following all the signs that said "airport" but he tried to take a short cut and deviated from all the signs and we saw a garbage truck that suddenly blocked our path and the car that was behind us stopped right behind us very close and those two to three seconds before the garbage truck moved, all of us lost our breath thinking the worst. After recuperating, our breaths we kept going, and we saw that indeed it was a short cut.

The cab driver dropped us off at the entrance and looked for airline AeroMexico that supposedly my aunt Essie supposedly had bought the tickets from. When we found the ticketing booth my dad got in line and waited his turn then when he got to speak with the lady behind the desk, she told him there were no tickets bought, so we had to buy them with pesos and dollars we had, and the ticket totaled $1,200 dollars for all five of us. We bought them and headed to the security checkpoint where they redirected us with an immigration officer because Jonathan didn't have his ID and at first the guy didn't believe us so he wanted to ask him a few questions privately.

He was reluctant to believe his story, so Jonathan then started to talk and respond in English and ended up giving him another ID; the same one given to us at the repatriation center. When we were done there, Jonathan and Ruber went to the place where they check the bags through a scanner while my dad went to go get our tickets. I went to call Maria, but since I didn't have enough change, only about a minute of time, I quickly gave the flight information to her and told her to call Pablo or Rubria so they can pass the information to someone in Guadalajara. Our flight information was departing from Tijuana on flight #111 at 10:00 A.M. and arriving in Guadalajara at 3:00 P.M. It was a three-hour flight with a two-hour difference due to daylight savings. When I called her, it was barely 7:00 A.M., so we went to eat breakfast at the local diner and waited for our flight to depart. When we went in the plane, and sat at our designated seats. I could see in all of our faces a sense of relief yet uncertainty of what's to come. The flight attendant came down the aisle asking what kind of drinks we wanted. My dad said water, my mom said water, my two brothers said water and when she asked me I said, "Whiskey on the rocks" and my parents and brothers turned their heads slowly to look at me and I said, "We're not in handcuffs anymore;" then they all changed their drinks to soda and juices. It felt really good to fly without handcuffs and chains.

Two days later on October 29, 2010, we left Tijuana and headed to Guadalajara. I couldn t believe after so long I was getting closer and closer to the city that saw my birth. if I hadn't been deported at all for about a couple of months, it would've been twenty years of not going back to see my native land. Even though I was with my parents and brothers throughout this whole ordeal, the separation from my wife and my daughter left a bitter taste of the way I felt about the United States. I was the breadwinner of my household, who will feed my kids now?

Alyssa Marie Messina, three months old, left without a father

Joel Alexander Messina, six years old, left without a father

When we landed in Guadalajara, we exited the plane, passed baggage claim because none of us had suitcases and went straight to a taxi. My dad asked for a van because it was five of us and regular taxis were Nissan Taurus, which were four-passenger cars versus a van had more room. My dad told the taxi conglomerate we needed to go to the Monumental neighborhood, which is across town, but nobody wanted to take us until my dad told one of them to take us to San Juan de Dios, which is a famous market center in the heart of the Plaza Tapatia, and he was kind enough to drive us there.

When we took that drive from the airport, we were kind of joking around of how fast we got to where we were going without hitting something. One day we the five of us were living our lives in five different ways and the next day we were faced with the same destination... deportation. We were looking outside the van window as we were talking and reminiscing when we noticed the housing projects surrounding the airport outskirts where not even done. Everything in Mexico is made from either brick or concrete blocks and then painted over, but these houses were just made from brick and never finished, like a brick house poorly constructed without inspection.

Also the streets didn't have asphalt or concrete, just plain dirt roads, and when it rained, it left manholes unattended. I believe all five of us were in one way or another thinking the same thoughts as we kept looking outside. As you're driving, you have to figure out which lane you're going on because when the white lane lines get faded they aren't repainted for quite some time.

The houses—it didn't matter if it was a nice one or a low-income one—are all structured the same way: one right next to another one without any space in between them.

On top of that it's like living in a birdcage. They all have to have steel bars to keep intruders from breaking into your homes. The trajectory we did from the airport to my grandmother's house was about forty-five minutes long, but it seemed about two hours due to the fact our future looked like a big enigma. We didn't have clothes or nothing to our name that we could come home to and change or organize, just the clothes we had from our deportation two days ago. The car payments, the mortgage, our bills, the gym memberships all gone.

When we got near San Juan de Dios, my dad asked the taxi driver if he could take us to a couple of blocks away from Jalisco Stadium, and he would give him a tip. The driver agreed. The cab driver set forth to the new destination closer to my grandmother's house that saved us a lot of walking. As we were going down the Calzada Independencia road, I started to remember bits and pieces from my childhood here, but everything looked so changed. When we got to grandma's house my dad gave the driver $20 pesos for tip ($1.50 dollars) and the driver looked at the change in his hands and had the look like he expected more and didn't even say thank you and when we got off, he sped off and started our walk towards grandma's house.

My aunt Mona came out first, and from everything that was going on, it took her a while to open the front door, which had a double lock, and then the outer gate also was double locked. When she finally got everything opened we gave each other a twenty-year hug along with my grandmother who I haven't seen in over ten years. As soon as my mom hugged my grandmother, she started crying and we all felt emotional, but not enough to cry. I guess you can say we were dehydrated from weeping for two days straight.

By this time it was about 3:00 P.M. to 4:00 P.M., and my grandmother had ordered chicken from a place that delivers.

After we ate and settled down, we started to tell them about the odyssey we were just in since ICE picked us up on the morning of October 27 up until we got to their front door. My cousin Cristian had gone to the airport to look for us and my aunt had called him back 'cause we'd arrived

Picture taken by my wife Maria at her parents' house in Galt, California. We would chat and have Alyssa next to her.

In Mexico there are places where you can go use the internet for a fee called "cyber cafés," which are usually from three to about ten computers in a room and charge about fifty cents to a dollar an hour. My dad had sent me to this cyber café down the street to let everybody know in the States we were okay. I kept in contact via email back and forth, so they knew what was going on with us and our progress in Mexico. In the States you hear about the violence in Mexico and the insecurity that dwells everywhere you go, so for the first months, there we were, scared even to go to buy a gallon of milk down the street to the store 'cause we felt like we were followed everywhere we went. It was the paranoia kicking in from watching too much TV in the States.

The family we had in Guadalajara specially my cousin Hiram and his brothers went all out when it came to helping us like getting our documents in order to finding jobs. When they knew about our deportation, they came early the next morning and dropped off some clothes in our grandma's driveway so we would have something to wear besides the same attire we have had since we got dropped off in Tijuana by ICE. One of the things my cousin Hiram did was ask my dad what kind of shoe size he was. He told my dad to put his wicker-type sandals on to see if they fit him, and as my dad was taking of his shoes to see if in fact it did fit him, my cousin got inside his vehicle without his sandals and told him "they are yours" and drove off.

It was a touching moment because we were not used to this level of kindness where someone literally takes off their shoes to give them to you. Our emotions were running on the surface so much to the point I almost hit my brother twice because of arguments about stupid things we siblings have about certain topics. I can't remember what the topic was off the top of my head, but it didn't matter when it came to arguing or debating, my brother excelled even if I was right and he was wrong.

I kept thinking about the life we all used to have and how one day it was changed completely, from all of us having jobs and studying to throwing us out without thinking the damage it causes. My mom at one point told us it's okay to cry and vent if we needed to and there's no shame in that. We went through a lot and we have to learn to adapt but adaptation comes with dealing with one's feelings first. I couldn't live with my brother Ruber anymore, we would bump heads a lot, so for the sake of our friendship I decided to move out. I asked my uncle Oscar if I could live with him for some time while I look for a job and get settled in. His house was in the Oblatos neighborhood close to where we had our old house where I was raised as a little kid before emigrating to the states.

While we were coping to adaptation in Guadalajara our houses in Oakley which were at one point filled with smiles and laughter were now vacant and about to go into foreclosure. The house my dad was renting was being emptied by friends and relatives and my house was soon to follow the same fate. One of the things I was very angry at was the way the United States government very stupidly handles these types of situations. For instance, how come when we were being deported, they didn't stop and looked at how we were living? Didn't they know we had employees and were paying taxes? Didn't they for one second stopped and looked at my brothers lives and saw they were academic scholars. They also didn't know I left my electrical engineering class halfway through and was about two to three months away from achieving my black belt in martial arts.

When my brother Ruber told me the teachers at Los Medanos College wanted him to be a tutor, but he told them he couldn't because he was undocumented and the school's response was "we don't care, we'll pay you under the table" it's got to count for something., Now what you're going to have here is an empty space, an empty space where a family could've paid taxes, could've spent money to help the economy grow. They just come and throw you to the other side without thinking of the outcome in all angles. None of my family members or myself had ever been in jail or be put in a position of this kind. We weren't the best, but we striving to be, weren't the worst to deserve this treatment and humiliation.

We became another number in the statistical spreadsheet of the Obama administration strategically in place to separate families. Obama promised he would stop the raids, but to make a few faces smile in his opposite party and make them happy we were dragged into it.

By the time everything was out of my dad's house, everyone did an outstanding job. Everyone in my family that day did exceptional work, though, when it came to my house, only a couple maybe a few more came through and helped. I was a bit upset because no one came to my house and those who did, did it with a little bit of energy. Later my uncle Pablo told my dad that by the time they came to my house, they were fatigued, which was understandable, but it was frustrating knowing my wife and daughter were alone without the help they needed from both my family and hers. Sometimes it takes something of this magnitude to know for sure who's with you.

My wife's family was supposed to be there and to my understanding they were only there a day maybe two and not all of them. I can't really say a lot about this whole fiasco because we couldn't be there to see what went on, but I do appreciate everybody that was a part of it and helped us until the end. All the friends that I supposedly had were all a lie, especially some friends that I had since high school who I considered my closest. Ruben, our most loyal worker who had been with us since we started Messina's Landscaping, helped until everything was moved and for his loyalty and support we gave him our 1990 Ford 150 as a token of our appreciation.

My dad had contacted my uncle Miguel from Los Angeles when we were in Tijuana to see if he would let us rent his house in Zapopan which is next to Guadalajara. The house was a couple streets down from the Benito Juarez Auditorium home of the Fiestas de Octubre. My uncle told my dad there was no need to give him any monetary installment, just to go get the keys from his brother-in-law and to be at the house until we see fit. While I was living with my uncle Oscar, I started to look for work. It was kind of hard, but I remember different people telling me if you knew English it wouldn't be that difficult to find work.

We applied for the IFE card (Electoral Federal Institute card) which is the most important ID in Mexico. They took about a month to process and get back to us. After we had the IFE card, we went to the transit building, which is equivalent to the DMV in the States, we got our driver's license, which was an easy process since my cousin Hiram Messina was the manager overseeing all driver's licenses and knew of our situation.

Everyone around him was sympathetic and helped us do the exams. My brothers didn't even have to take the written exams because they didn't know Spanish that well so one of my cousin's aides told them to step aside while he just clicked on the screen and did the test for them. When I was doing the written exam in Spanish, I found out how little I knew of the correct grammar and wording used. I passed with a 75 percent and felt lucky. The driving part I was so nervous because in the States they take you out to the roads and have you drive in live traffic and coincidentally when we were arriving at the DMV for these tests there had been a car accident in front of us, not a serious one but enough to think twice before driving in a new environment where the car, not the pedestrian has the right of way.

When it was my turn to do the driving test, I saw they don't even take you outside to the city streets. All you do is go around the facility parking lot and do a stop and park and pretty much give you the okay. This is how easy it is to get a driver's license in Mexico; all you need to do is learn the language and get the right paperwork and you practically have a driver's license. My brother Ruber didn't even know how to turn on a car when he did the driving part of the exam and he has one—until this day he has never used his drivers license (it doesn't matter what year you read this part of the book, he never will).

As soon as we arrived in Guadalajara on October 29, 2010, within a month we already had a recent birth certificate, driver's license, and the IFE card, which are all the requisites to obtain a job. The only thing needed was a resume and the will to go hunt for a job. My cousin Danny from Canada and his girlfriend at the time Vanessa were living in Guadalajara in the downtown area off of Juarez street. He asked us for our resumes so he could submit them to their human resources department and see if he could get us in where he worked.

Our other cousins the Messina Sanchez clan where keeping an ear open for possible jobs we could get and one of the interviews my brother Jonathan and I went to was a call center called Teletech. My cousins heard this through the radio and said they needed fluent speakers for customer service purposes.

These jobs are meant to outsource jobs in the United States in which all made sense now. The United States starts deporting people and then companies overseas get a lot of influx of deportees find these jobs because these people like us already know the culture and how to reel in the customer and take advantage of that $5-a-day minimum wage in Mexico.

Whenever you call almost any big corporation in the US that has a 1-800 number you might be talking to your neighbor next door who was deported and the only job this person could take in Mexico is a call center job because of the high bilingual demand and low-paying jobs that pay a little bit more than your average job in Guadalajara, but it's still low enough to make a corporation rich in the United States.

While we looked for a job my cousin Danny worked at the Mayan Monday through Friday, and then some Saturdays we would go to his pad and his girlfriend would show us around. My brother Jonathan and I thought it was funny a Canadian was showing us the city where we were born. One day we started walking towards the downtown area and we were handed a pamphlet saying if we wanted to be an extra in a movie called *Mariachi Gringo*, and I told my brother to go and sign up for the hell of it.

We followed the lady who gave us the pamphlet into the lobby of a nice hotel in the downtown area where they took our information while they measured our weight and height. They said if they selected us, they would contact us by November 18 and start filming by December 13. We didn't pay much attention to it because there are so many beautiful people in Guadalajara why would they pick us, right? We did it for the fun of it, we had nothing to lose.

My uncle Oscar would invite us frequently to his house for some drinks and appetizers, and one night, he let my dad borrow a car he had and used seldom; it was a Gulf Volkswagen. This car was the sorriest car you've ever seen; it had no shocks and in Mexico having a car with no shocks is like walking in the dessert with shoes and no socks. Sure you'll get to where you're going, but eventually your feet are going to need some medical attention.

On our way back to our grandmother's house, I hit a speed bump and when I say I hit a speed bump probably going five miles an hour and the bottom of the car hit the bump, and it turned off as I was going over it. My dad yelled at me and said I was going too fast (I should've gone 4 miles an hour now that I think about it), but the reality of the problem was it was five of us in this little no-shock vehicle. My brother Ruber alone weighed more than 250 pounds, so you can imagine us all like sardines in this little hatchback going over a speed bump. As we were getting out of the car to push, it must've been close to midnight. We didn't know if we wanted to laugh or cry. I reminded everybody about the time not even a month ago from this day if they remembered when we went to celebrate my mom's birthday to a Japanese restaurant in Brentwood.

My mom got upset and left walking. We pushed the car about three blocks, our lives did a 180 and changed like if you changed the channels on a television.

On the weekends we would go to the Huentitan Mountain to walk, some people would run or jog and others just by walking was exercise enough. I was still fresh in my training and my jogging and remember taking about an hour to walk downwards and half an hour to jog it upwards. People who suffer heart conditions are recommended not to try it because the slopes are steep, and it's far enough that if you were to have a heart attack, there's no way to bring you up unless someone with an extreme physique carries you.

When Thanksgiving week came around, we have some relatives in Livermore, California whom every year they spend it by going on a cruise but with this tragedy within our family, they didn't feel comfortable in taking that trip and instead decided to come to Guadalajara to spend it with us and to bring us some of our stuff we had in California. Especially my brother Ruber who was six feet two inches tall, and when it came time to buy him clothes or shoes, it was a hassle. The biggest sizes you find in Guadalajara was 2XL which was XL in the States, and he was 2XL in the states which translated to 3XL or sometimes, even 4XL in Mexico and was rarely heard of.

Whenever a family member came from the States, they would come for the sole purpose to help us regain our stuff so we didn't have to spend money on something we already have. My aunt Dinora from Wisconsin sent us used laptops and my aunt Eva from Livermore sent my mom money to pay for the internet so we could be connected via email and SKYPE with everybody and wouldn't have to go to the cyber cafés anymore. My uncle Pablo sold my dad his '96 Nissan Pickup so my dad could have a decent vehicle to drive. My uncle Jesus from San Jose drove the truck to the border where a company brought it to Guadalajara. My cousin Hiram helped my dad and me in picking up the truck because he knew all the legal jargon in Mexico and helped us with identifying the paperwork.

In order to lift us our spirits—which by this point were still pretty low but with everything going on in looking for a job and trying to fit into a Mexican society—we were invited to a family gathering in the Tabachines neighborhood of Guadalajara. They had a small inflatable pool for the kids, a DJ, food, and a variety of drinks. In that gathering our Messina Sanchez cousins told us what else can they do in their part to get us going with jobs and if there was anything else they can do to let them know. Thanks to them, both of my brothers were able to get jobs in Teletech which was located in the southern part of Guadalajara.

Both my brother and I had the interview with Teletech on December 4, 2010 at the same time but because he lived with my parents at my grandmother's house, and I lived with my uncle Oscar, we took the same subway train at different times. In the interview they give you simple questions as to how did you learn your English and where do you live, after they give you two or three protocol questions, which don't matter, they ask you when can you start if they were to hire you. I told them I could start January 17, 2011 because my wife and daughter were going to come on December 26 for three weeks, and I wanted to be there since I hadn't seen them in over a month and a half.

They accepted my condition if I was to start working there, and I left with a positive feeling that there were good chances that I would get the job since the most important quality they cared for is the knowledge of the English language.

The following day while I checked my email on the computer, I overheard my aunt Norma arguing with my cousin Valeria downstairs. My aunt had left to drop off Valeria at school walking and when they came back is when I heard them argue. What had happened is since we're so close to Christmas all the scum of society starts to creep out and crime starts to kick in full gear. My cousin Valeria had a bag who in my aunt's eyes was too flagrant, and it would be attracting would be thieves.

My aunt claims they were followed and returned home to leave in the car but asked my cousin to leave the purse home since she would be walking home when school ended. I offered to go with them since I wasn't doing anything at the time, but my aunt declined the offer and said they would leave by car. Later that day my aunt and I had a conversation about why I wanted to leave to the States and not live in Mexico since it was a great country with lots of potential to which I responded that Mexico will always have a warmth place in my heart because it gave me a blanket when the United States took it from me by force and the only reason I would choose not live there was the fact that I wouldn't feel comfortable to tell my daughter every time Christmas was around the corner to not go out with her favorite purse because she would be in danger of being in harm's way. It does happen in the States but only in very large metropolis areas that we were not accustomed to. That's why we never were in a large city.

And even though Guadalajara is a large metropolis, we wouldn't be able to settle in anywhere else in Mexico because the jobs were scarce, and that pushes people to go to the big cities or immigrate north. I was just used to the life I was living in the States and my aunt was used to the life in Mexico.

Another incident that happened while I was living with my uncle was a phone call I received from my cousin Brian who wanted me to pick him up from the airport. I didn't answer the phone my aunt did and told him I wasn't going to be able to pick him up because I didn't own a car. I told her it was very strange to me because Brian and I don't speak since some years back, and even if it was him and he asked me to go pick him up, I wouldn't have done it. After a couple of hours this so called "Brian" claiming to be my cousin called again, and I answered and he said if our aunt had told me about the airport situation, and as I heard his voice, I knew it wasn't him and hung up the phone.

My aunt told me that extortionists use this method to kidnap people and get money out of the families. Sometimes the airport employees sell the information to third parties known for their criminal activities or listen to you on your cell phone when you're on the bus or walking down the street and get you that way, my first kidnapping experience, dodged that bullet. The following week my uncle Oscar asked me if I wanted to go to Maeva with them. Maeva is an all-inclusive hotel and resort by the city of Manzanillo, Colima in Miramar Beach. They make the trip every year as a family for about three or four nights. What happened was one of my cousins couldn't go, and since it was for her and her husband, they invited my parents but my parents didn't feel like taking a trip so soon because the deportation was still too recent so they passed.

When they asked me, even though I was third in line, I was very grateful and said yes for two reasons. First of all, I didn't know Mexico; the only thing I knew for the last two months was Guadalajara, and second of all, living in the States, the only two decent beaches I knew were Miami and Hawaii and they both don't compare to being in a Mexican beach. I'll never forget that weekend in December where I spent it in a resort where I was able to eat, sleep, and swim at any time of the day, like they say here in the States "priceless." When we came back from Maeva, my mom gave me the news that her brother Uncle Mario wanted us to spend Christmas with them in Guayabitos, Nayarit.

I didn't know where it was but it sounded like a magical place, and it was. We stayed in a bungalow right off the beach, which is about a little bit more than an hour north of Puerto Vallarta. My dad didn't want to go because he didn't want to leave my grandmother by herself, so my mom said if my brothers and I say yes, she'll go, but if we say no, she won't go. When she asked us if we wanted to go, we were already packed before she could even finish the sentence.

A couple of weeks before the Christmas trip, I had received a call at my grandmother's house regarding being an extra in the movie *Mariachi Gringo* and my mom gave them the number to my uncle's house so they could tell me about it. They called me to tell me they want to cast me as an extra. I got excited because I've been a big movie fan in the States. I used to go to the movies a lot, and now to get a chance to be in it, even though it's just for a little bit was mesmerizing. The guy on the other side of the phone told me to be in the neighborhood of "las nueve esquinas" or the nine corners in the morning and to dress all in black because I was going to play a bouncer at a bar. When I got there, they told me they needed a copy of my IFE card so they could pay me. While I was getting the paperwork ready at a local cyber café, I saw they were doing takes in an alley with the actors and a mariachi.

One of the guys who was also an extra started to talk to me, and through him I found out the main actor was Shawn Ashmore. I didn't know who he was, and he was shocked. I told him I'm not good at recognizing people, and then he told me if I had seen the movie *X-Men* and said the mutant that has the power of creating ice was Shawn Ashmore. The assistant director was the same one that did the Mexican show "La Academia." I guess it must've been TV, but Shawn Ashmore looked way to skinny to be an X-Men.

There was a lot of waiting around but the good thing is they served us a buffet-like style in an abandon house they were using as a prop in the movie.

When it came time to film my part for the movie the assistant casting director took me to the scene which was a bar off the Plaza Tapatia called "La Fuente" and when we got there, the cameras where already leaving. He had taken me too late so when we came back for the last scene of the day that was by a fountain in front of the main cathedral in Guadalajara called "La Catedral," the casting director told me if I had different clothes, and I said they told me to come all black for the scene I just missed. I ended up being in the background of the water fountain scene in which Sean Ashmore is sitting on the steps looking straight at the camera.

It took about forty-five minutes to an hour and about ten takes to get the shot right. Our job is to walk around and tell the people who were passing by not to stare directly at the camera. After it was over, they took us back to that hotel lobby where they first gathered our information to pay us in cash. I received $500 pesos ($40 dollars) cash, which was kinda cool to have worked only for an hour. I saw the movie sometime later after it came out and I appear for about five seconds.

Christmas came around, and it was time to go to Guayabitos with my uncle Mario. We left in two cars; my uncle Mario drove his SUV and I drove his Ford Ranger crew cab. My grandfather was hesitant to let me drive because he said I didn't have enough experience to drive in Mexican roads, but my mom convinced him at the end that it was all right and I could drive in any terrain. After four and a half hours of driving in curves and whatnot, my grandfather was satisfied that I could drive in Mexico anywhere.

I had mixed feelings about that Christmas year, mixed because every day in Guayabitos I was in shorts and sandals whereas in California you wouldn't be caught near anywhere that had to do with swimming unless it was in a Jacuzzi or heated pool. It was the first time without my dad, and it felt different. It was the first time in twenty years my mom spent Christmas with her family, and she looked super happy. Those moments were embedded in my memory forever. My uncle Mario took his new wife Aide along with his new in-laws and had us all in bungalows three blocks from the main downtown area.

It was those little towns you see in the travel channel that are full of humility and rich in culture and knowing the fact I was right there relaxing with a couple of beers made it unforgettable. It was a weird Christmas because of the environment, but the heat and the beach made it mystical, and I'm glad I went. We were in Mexico for two months and everybody was supportive and attentive, a quality we hadn't seen in our family from up north until we got deported. We ended up cutting the trip short because my wife Maria and my brother's girlfriend where to arrive in Guadalajara on December 26.

We took a bus in the town of La Peñita on December 25, and my grand-father drove us to our meeting point. We took a taxi from the Tlaquepaque central bus station to my uncle Oscar's house to have a dinner with his family for Christmas, and my dad was already waiting for us. It was a very elegant dinner where everybody wore their finest attire. The table was very carefully decorated with my aunt's finest china and the turkey was juicy and very delicious.

My cousin Hiram had let me borrow his van for the time my wife was in town to take them out, which was a very nice for him to do for us. The next three weeks to come were really like a vacation, and we had some good quality time as a family. My daughter Alyssa looked so big after two months of not being with her. She looked taller and had changed so much since the last time I got to glance at her at the detention center in San Francisco. I remember holding her, and since she wasn't used to me, she started to cry for her mom, but I didn't care. It felt like when you lose something valuable and after some time you find it. I didn't want to let go; her crying was like music to my ears. Never thought I would say that.

For New Years of 2010 into 2011, Maria and I dropped off Jonathan and his girlfriend at Club Cherry Lobby in Guadalajara, and we went off to my parents' compadres restaurant where we had dinner and saw the fireworks the kids in the street were playing with. Everywhere in Guadalajara, there was something going on in every street I've never seen a metropolis so engaged in party mode not even when I visited New York a few years back. we visited so many places probably more than ever when we were here. We went to the fol-lowing cities and towns, in the state of Jalisco: Tonala, Tlaquepaque, Ama-cueca, Sayula, San Gabriel, Chapala, Tequila; in the state of Colima: Colima, Cuyutlan, Manzanillo; in the state of Nayarit: Rincon de Guayabitos. In Guayabitos we stayed about a couple of blocks down from where our uncle Mario had taken us for Christmas.

Picture taken by my wife Maria at the all-inclusive Decameron Resort in Rincón de Guayabitos, Nayarit taken the first week of January of 2011.

When my brother's girlfriend and Maria left, I had mentally prepared myself to go back to job hunting. By this time, we had already planned to change lawyers or look for someone else because this lawyer had told my wife there was nothing she could do and to deal with it. My wife was resilient and didn't give up on my return. January 17, 2011 came around, and it was time for them to leave and just when my daughter started to feel comfortable around me, destiny was going to take her again, back to reality. We said our goodbyes at Miguel Hidalgo y Costilla International airport in Guadalajara and the next day I gave my cousin back his van. I cried myself to sleep the night they left after I punched the concrete wall as hard as I could out of anger.

Technically I already had a job because Teletech had said they were going to call me back. I didn't receive a call back right away, but my cousin Danny told me to call Mayan Resorts because it's a better company than Teletech and there's more opportunity to grow whereas at Teletech I would be stuck doing the same thing. Since I wasn't getting a callback, I called the human resources department in Mayan and Irene Sanchez answered the phone and scheduled an appointment for us to meet.

She told me precisely the moment I called she was trying to decide which of us three of my brothers and I she was going to call because corporate rules states relatives can't work in the same department and since I called them ahead, I got the golden ticket for the opportunity. They scheduled the interview the last week of January and I dressed formal with a suit and tie, and driving a car that was going to disintegrate very soon, the famous Volkswagen Gulf that my uncle let us borrow.

When I got to Mayan headquarters, there were two interviewers, Irene whom didn't look older than me at all, probably midtwenties who did the interview in Spanish by asking simple questions like my marital status and how did I hear of them. The second interviewer was Robert, who was in charge of the national executive branch for Mayan Resorts and he wanted to interview by speaking English and was testing my vocal abilities, he asked me simple questions, but it looked like he didn't care at all just wanted to hear me speak. His accent is like any of those that learned how to speak English in Mexico. They told me they were going to contact me if I was the right candidate for the job and I left not knowing if I had the job or not.

Irene had told me if I did get it the job, it implied I was going to be transferred to Puerto Vallarta and since I never had been to Vallarta, I would welcome the opportunity. I've always had a soft spot in my heart for the beach ambience. Mayan Resorts called and let me know to come to their installations on January 31 2011 to sign the papers to start my training: myself and five more people. I later found out that two of us were from Guadalajara and the rest from Puerto Vallarta.

On that day they told us about the job and what it entailed, we signed papers for tax purposes and other insurance-related papers, and by February 1 we could consider ourselves International Executives at the contact center for Mayan Resorts. My parents were happy not so much of the job, but that I had a distraction instead of being home depressed. I decided to go to my uncle Miguel's house and leave my tio Oscar's house because it was more convenient for me to drive to work. I would drive from the Benito Juarez Auditorium to Calzada Federalismo all the way to Circunvalacion until I got to Lazaro Cardenas pass the Minerva Roundabout and behind the Grand Plaza was where Mayan used to be.

Mr. Carlos Morales or "Charles" as he was known, trained us for three weeks in Guadalajara and then passed the torch to Edgar "el chaparro" Elizarraras the last week of training in Puerto Vallarta. Those were four intense weeks because we had to learn many types of contracts for timeshare owners who typically wanted to leave their remote cold locations to spend some time in the nice warm temperatures the Mexican shoreline had to offer. This particularly timeshare was Mexican owned, but the managerial department was run by foreigners since the clientele demographic showed a lot of percentage owned by North Americans like Canadians and people in the US from the northern states.

When I started the training, they told me I was going to get paid $7,000.00 pesos ($540.00 dollars) on a monthly basis. ARE YOU KIDDING ME?! Did I hear correctly? I'm working for a company that charges customers in dollars, and I'm getting paid this amount on a monthly basis? I couldn't believe it. Charles could've told us a tidal wave was coming straight at us, and I wouldn't have paid attention I was so out of it. I thought about it all the way until I went to bed that night. I was making more at a McDonald's by the age of seventeen in 1997 than in a corporate office in Mexico.

Even as I write these lines it's unbelievable to think a company known worldwide had such unfair policies about employee payment but then again that's why the corporate office is in Mexico and not the United States. A girl in my group Veronica was telling me how excited she was as I took her to the pharmacy down the street because not everybody gets a chance to be in a company like this. As she told me that, I was telling her how utterly disappointed I was. I shouldn't have said anything because for someone in Mexico, it's a good paying job that I wasn't used to, but I still couldn't keep my mouth closed about the way it was set up.

I decided to go forward and keep going to the training besides I was going to live in Puerto Vallarta and you can say it was the main reason for giving the green light to that opportunity. While I trained in the Mayan, I kept in contact with my wife Maria through SKYPE and Yahoo Chat. Between Maria, her brother Mark, and our loyal worker Ruben whom never let us down in more than five years kept Messina's Landscaping afloat. Just in case there was a chance for me to come back soon and also to keep paying the mortgage on our house that took us so much effort to get before I got deported.

Because neither my dad nor myself were there to talk to the clients and meet up their landscape demands, Maria started to get too many complaints that she didn't know how to handle because she's not a landscaper and her brother, even though he knew how to do the job, there was a difference between mowing your own lawn and doing it as a business, Ruben didn't know English, so there was a communication barrier if he was to run the company by himself.

After a week or two of the same thing, I told Maria to send a letter to all the clients letting them know we were going to close Messina's Landscape and to thank them for their business. The truck used for the landscaping business was a white Toyota Tundra 2005 with lumber racks and a toolbox on the side. This truck was going to be sold, so my uncle had it, and since they were using Ruben's truck to do the landscaping, he kept telling Mark it wasn't well mechanically, so Maria got the sense that he didn't want us to use his truck for work which is understandable.

My brother Jonathan's girlfriend's dad knew what was going on with our company and told my wife one of his friends about it and they agreed to buy us the maintenance route for a thousand dollars. I told Maria to go ahead and do it since we're going to close the company we might as well get something out of it. I couldn't believe I was paying the employees in California more than I was getting paid in Guadalajara. I was paying them a hundred dollars a day and I was making a hundred dollars a week, wow, I couldn't believe it. By the time I was in training in Mayan, Messina's Landscaping was coming to an end in the Bay Area.

Three weeks in Guadalajra and the last one in Vallarta starting February 1, the six of us were Gabriela Palomo, Yesica Cruz, Veronica Lopez, Arnulfo Macias, Juan Romero, and yours truly. Everybody lived in Puerto Vallarta except Arnulfo or "Arnold" and I. The person in the group whom I had more in common was Juan because he also was deported and had lived in LA and Arizona. I even took him to my grandmother's house where my parents where living at the time to hang out. He went with me to the baratillo to buy clothes to take to Vallarta; the baratillo is a section in Guadalajara where there are blocks and blocks of tentlike street stores. They sell everything from clothes to electronic equipment. It's the biggest "tianguis" or flea market in Latin America.

My parents had bought four tickets to see a rock and roll group in the Plaza Tapatia and had originally invited my uncle Oscar and aunt Norma, but were unable to go. He asked me if I wanted to invite anybody to go watch the concert. They would give tribute to some of music's biggest names like Eydie Gormé, Santa Ana, and the Beatles. I decided to invite Juan, and after work we went straight to my grandmother's house where we all went together to the Degollado Theatre.

My mom gave me the tickets to hold and when we got to the theatre, I found out I didn't have them with me. Juan and I jumped into the car as quickly as we could and headed off to my grandmother's house in the Volkswagen Gulf via the Calzada Independencia street. When I crossed the street of Circunvalacion, I felt the clutch between first and second was acting up. Right before we were to cross the Jalisco Stadium, which was a couple of streets down from where my grandmother lived, the car stalled and it didn't want to turn on again. There was so much traffic and I had just made it worse so we got off and a transit cop pulled over to help us with the traffic while we pulled to the side.

There was a problem bigger than this whole ordeal, there was a game going on at the stadium which meant that for blocks and blocks either way there was going to be no parking whatsoever and the spots that were open for parking, the local people were standing outside next to them to charge other people who come and watch the game. Even though they saw me and Juan pushing from down the street, I asked if I could leave it overnight while I figure out what to do, but everybody threw me a price to park. After some blocks of pushing the car, we found an abandoned house and decided to leave it there.

I knocked on the house adjacent and a girl about sixteen years old came out, and I gave her my information in case the city or the owners came and tried towing it. Juan and I raced to my grandmother's house, which was about five blocks away to get the tickets and left in a taxi. The concert was off the hook. I've never been inside the Degollado Theatre and its celestial magnificence. As you step inside, you're stepping into a pre-colonial era with its rustic look engineered to awe at every angle. We were in the mezzanine in the upper level on the right side overlooking the rows in the bottom and the stage.

After the concert, we all walked to the Calzada Independencia street to look for a taxi and then decided to walk into a small diner to eat and then kept walking. We couldn't find a taxi; they were all full of concertgoers going home, so we decided to keep walking until we got home, which took about an hour. In my dad's Nissan truck, I took Juan to the Hotel Malibu, where everybody training that came from Vallarta was staying. The next day my dad, my brothers and I went to get the Volkswagen

Gulf from the abandoned house and pushed it back to my grandmother's between midday traffic.

By this time, it was around St. Valentines 2011 and Maria had said my cousin Adelita sent her the information for her lawyer in San Francisco, which helped her and her family achieve legal status and was very efficient. I spoke with my new lawyer Marcia a little bit on the phone, and it gave me a sense of confidence I hadn't felt in a while especially when I told her "if you get me back to the United States, I will personally go to the town of Tequila and buy you a bottle" to which she responded "don't worry I will end up drinking it." Maria and I decided to go forward and go into contract with her since our previous lawyer from Sacramento didn't do anything and sat on our case "finessing her work" for over three years without any results.

The end of the third week of training at Mayan headquarters in Guadalajara was coming and our trainer Charles said they would give Arnold and I a suite in the Sea Garden for two weeks while we find a place to stay. Later on we would found out if we were to stay in the same suite they would double our stay for four weeks. Sunday February 20 via ETN bus paid by Mayan Resorts, we left to Puerto Vallarta. My parents left me at the bus station, and I told them when I had a chance I would come and visit them.

They met Arnold who came almost simultaneously as we were getting there, and my mom said he looked Asian because Arnold was wearing a traditional Chinese bamboo hat and wore it all the way to Vallarta. I left my brother Jonathan my cellular phone because it had a Guadalajara area code of 331 so I wrote all the main contacts from Guadalajara and told my parents as soon as I get there, I was going to buy a phone with a Vallarta area code of 322 and text them the number. When the bus started to leave the bus station, I felt a little bit nostalgic because I was going to be completely on my own and was uncertain what destiny awaited me in Vallarta.

My mom was so worried about me leaving her side because I didn't know how to do anything. I didn't know how to wash clothes or even make myself dinner unless it was cereal or opening a can of tuna. I lived under my parents' roof until I got married and then when I moved out and then got married, my wife continued the tradition of making me useless when it came to house chores. It was a positive move because I felt I grew emotionally and learned to live on my own and now that I keep having those luxuries, I don't take them for granted.

I left my family and Guadalajara, which I was starting to call my home but not for one second did I hesitate in thinking it was a bad move. I left with my chin up high and an open mind to explore the Jalisco coastline. Arnold and I arrived in Puerto Vallarta that Sunday afternoon as the sun set on the horizon, so beautiful with its palm trees along the beaches. The bus we went in had free wi-fi, a television in each seat with headphones and you could either listen to music or watch a movie. We took a taxi to Nuevo Vallarta into the Mayan Sea Garden where our residency for the next month would be.

Myself and Arnold (Chino) Macias Torres eating a hamburger outside the Mayan Sea Garden

Living in a hotel was paradise. I've never stayed in one for more than a week and it was when we went to Hawaii for our honeymoon so being there for a month was euphoric. People would do your bed, leave chocolates under the pillow, room service, by the time I was clocking out, I was already relaxed and ready to go home. We had a city view in the fifth floor and our work was a ten-minute walk from the hotel. The room was a one-bedroom suite with a full kitchen and a sofa bed in the living room with a very small balcony, so small only people with a medium build physique could lodge themselves and wiggle into the balcony space.

I made a deal with Arnold for one of us to stay in the bedroom for two weeks and the other one for the remaining two, but he didn't mind staying in the living room for a month. I bought a Tequila bottle in the town of Tequila and the first week we were there we drank it to toast to our new job and new beginning. We would be at the beach all the time either enjoying the sun or playing soccer and only once we went in the pool.

The reservations department at the Contact Center for Mayan Resorts. On the right with blue shirt is Juan Romero Acamapitzin and opposite of him is supervisor Edgar Elizarraras.

The contact center for Mayan Resorts was situated on the first two levels of the resorts parking garage for valet parking. It was also an employee parking lot if you get the special permit that you apply for at the human resources department. It was a five-level parking in which the first two where the corporate office and all of its individual departments that ran Mayan Resorts in conjunction with Guadalajara. We went in through two security doors where we had to put our finger and a laser reader would verify who we were and then let us in.

We would pass the secretary area where it looked like a lobby area where it had a couple of couches if you were waiting for someone and then go through the accounting department, turn to the left and through the carpeted hallway through a double glass door where again you would put your index finger and into the contact center. The training room was the first one on your left, and then the main hub that hosted all of the computers to handle incoming and outgoing phone calls.

Edgar would finish our training for the next week and then off to the floor to answer calls. The contact center had five departments that intertwined each other to make it happen: the reservations area was the area designed to take incoming calls and make reservations; member services was the area designed to receive incoming calls also but its main purpose was to explain to the member a section of the contract he or she was having difficult grasping or where angry members would call because they were promised something they couldn't get through the reservation department. The inventory department was made so if there was a day or a check-in date we didn't see in our table of availability, they would try and see if they could open it up so we could get that reservation and make the customer happy.

Back office was intended to find discrepancies in our reservations or address an error in a contract. Finally, the quality control room which oversees all the contact center through windows and had the power to report anything from an abusive call to take points off of our evaluation, approve if we needed to leave early or when our vacation time came about.

I came into an OXXO store which were little seven eleven type stores you see in almost every corner throughout the state to buy a phone with a 322 area code chip. I immediately called my dad so he'd have my new number to keep in touch. The last two weeks we stayed at the Mayan Sea Garden we would barely start looking for a place to live and it was hard since we were the rookies of the contact center they would make us work every Saturday, which left us to look for a place on Sundays and most apartment buildings didn't open on Sundays or if we would find one suitable the owners where out and about.

We usually would search for a place near the downtown area because its where all the action was, bars, clubs, and tourist spots along with the Vallarta sunset. We couldn't find a decent place we liked, even though we literally would walk street by street, everything was either expensive or too small for two people to live in. We got to a store with a sign reading "information about apartments ask inside." We told the store lady we were interested and she immediately called another lady and let us know she was on her way to meet us.

Fifteen minutes must've passed by and we finally told the lady we would come another day, and she said the other lady was just around the corner. A lady showed up in a van with two kids a boy and a girl between the ages of eight and six. We asked the location of the apartment and she said it was in the "playa grande" neighborhood and then we proceeded to ask if it was close to the beach and she said "yes about twenty minutes." She would take us in her van to go look at it so we agreed and hopped on. Instead of going towards or near the beach we started to drive more and more towards the opposite direction towards the hills. All of a sudden, we weren't driving on asphalt or concrete anymore but dirt road still going deep and deep inland, and I started to feel uneasy about where this was headed and by the look on Arnold's face, he didn't like it one bit either.

I was still anxious about looking at the place and so was Arnold who knows what if it's a hidden paradise so we decided to give it a try. Then after a little bit of more driving on the dirt road, the houses didn't even looked fully built. They were all brick or missing sections, and we started to see goats and chickens on the streets just walking everywhere freely. The place looked like those places where they film commercial stating if you want to help a child for 10 cents a day because they're leaving in poor conditions and life expectancy is twelve years old etc., etc. Right before literally going up the hill we stopped and showed us the three rooms she had for $120 dollars a month. These rooms were so miserable I couldn't believe someone would actually consider living there.

This is how bad these rooms were when she opened one of the rooms a bat came flying out and scared the shit out of us. There wasn't enough room to really call it a home. It looked like a small studio with walls in itself to make it look like a micro apartment. The toilet was next to the shower head so you can be sitting in the toilet while taking a shower at the same time, convenient if you want to save time. Probably with about three or four giant steps you could go around the apartment a couple of times. I told the lady we would keep her number and if we decided to live here, we would give her a call. I whispered to Arnold without the lady hearing me that I would never ever ever ever ever ever ever in my life want to come here again even if it was Halloween.

When we were driving back and started to see civilization again, she said she would drop us off in front of the Walmart because she was going to purchase some groceries and left us in front of the Macroplaza. We took a bus to wherever because we didn't know where we were and as soon as we started seeing familiar streets we got off and took another one back to the Sea Garden.

On our ride back to the Sea Garden we were reminiscing on the trip we just did with the lady, and Arnold and I were thinking the same thing. We both thought we were going to get sequestered and or robbed. We both kid around the fact we were simultaneously going to open the door while the van was moving and throw ourselves out and run like hell. The last week a couple of friends from work Mauro and Martin asked Arnold if he wanted to go rent with them for the price of $125 dollars a month and then another coworker Pablo who was in charge of computer troubleshooting told me he would rent me a room for $85 dollars a month.

March 23, 2011 was our last day in the Mayan Sea Garden and Arnold left with Mauro and Martin and I left to Pablo's house, which was a couple of blocks down the street in the town of Valle Dorado, Nayarit. Around the first week of April, I told the supervisor if he would give me a ride to the house since he lived close by. He said he first needed to go to Galerias Vallarta for an errand, so if I wanted to go with him, he could do it.

Galerias Vallarta is Puerto Vallartas mall located in the marina in front of where all the cruise ships dock when they come from the United States. I thought about it for a little bit and then decided not to go with him. Instead I would take a "combi" or minivan, which where several ground transports that for a little bit more than a bus but took you to a specific location. I walked by the Mayan Sea Garden and got on a minivan and within ten minutes, I was at the Walmart in front of Valle Dorado. It's usually about a fifteen-minute walk to the house and today it would take almost an hour.

As I stepped off the minivan, I sprained my ankle. As I placed my left foot on the ground I miscalculated and put my whole weight on my ankle and heard five or six loud cracks. It sounded like when someone cracks all of their fingers, but it all came from my ankle. I started to move my foot in a clockwise and then counterclockwise rotation and at first it felt like it was helping, though I was limping a little bit. After about twenty or thirty steps, I had to sit down. The pain was so intense if the sole of my shoe would touch the ground a little bit, I felt like someone was stabbing my ankle mercilessly with sharp needles.

I started to panic because I could not walk home, so I called my roommate Pablo to see if he would come and pick me up, but there was no answer. I started to walk by kind of hopping on one foot] and sometimes I would try and walk with both feet but after a couple of steps the pain would get unbearable and would have to turn to hopping again. I finally got home, changed and walked over to Mauro, Martin and Arnold's pad, and Pablo was there.

When I told them what had happened, Pablo asked me how come I didn't call him, and I told him I did, but there was no answer. Mauro looked at my ankle and told me it looked bad so he went to his room got me one of his socks filled it with ice and rapped it around my ankle. After sitting down for an hour, I got up to leave, but I couldn't touch the floor again and my ankle had swollen to the size of a tennis ball, I had never seen anything like it, so Pablo took me home in his car. On the morning Pablo took me to the doctor and gave me medical leave for three days and some painkillers. I came out of the doctors in a wheelchair from the backside of the clinic.

We stopped around the corner to buy crutches and left me at his house while he went to work and did the favor of giving my supervisor the proper paperwork for the medical leave. I found myself struggling to do the simplest things like going to the kitchen or taking a shower so the cast doesn't get wet. The three days I rested went by in slow motion because I literally couldn't do anything. The day of my next appointment I went outside the house to see if there was a taxi to take me to the clinic, but there was nothing in sight.

I started to walk with the crutches I bought and after two blocks, a woman who saw me offered to give me a lift to the Walmart, between the Walmart and the house there was a long stretch of nothing but barren land for about half a mile. When I walked the rest of the way to the clinic, I developed blisters under my armpits from the crutches but fortunately I was able to get a taxi back to the house.

The doctor had given me another seven days of pay without work and as soon as I got out of my appointment, I took a taxi back to the house and told the taxi driver not to turn off his car while I got my things and then headed off to the Mezcales bus station where I would buy my ticket to Guadalajara. Because this was in April when spring break was in full throttle, on my way to Guadalajara it was just the bus driver and myself while the whole city of Guadalajara was trying to enter Puerto Vallarta.

The bus driver and I began conversing to the point I ended up sitting at the very front for practical reasons. I told him about my deportation and that I might have to go to Juarez for an interview and wanted his opinion on which was better if by plane or by bus. His honest response concluded my decision to go by plane. He told me even though his main income is by driving the bus and always tells everyone going by bus is safe, he advised me if I was going to take a trip to the northern states to go by plane because in the northern and eastern part of the country the cartels had taken over a lot of the terrain and it would be safer for me to travel by plane.

He told me a story that happened to him some time back when he went to the state of Tamaulipas, which borders Texas, where two or three black Suburbans cut in front of him and made him pull to the side and stopping the bus completely. Some men with machine guns came into the bus nabbed seven people and took them with them never to be seen again. He never knew if they were strategically or randomly chosen. I gave him my most sincere thanks for giving me the information and kept talking about different topics while we got to the bus station in Zapopan.

My parents were waiting for me at the bus station; I could see them through the bus window, and as I exited the bus, they were watching me step off with crutches their expression of worry began to unfold. I told them there was nothing to worry about. I happened to step off a transit van off the wrong foot and hurt my ankle, but I should be fine within a week or so. That particular week in Guadalajara was so relaxing. It was great. I didn't have to worry about making reservations, fixing reservations, or taking calls all day long. After the week passed, I went back to Vallarta and the doctor gave me another week, so I returned to Guadalajara for another week of relaxation.

The second time we went back, instead of going by bus, my dad decided to let me borrow a Nissan pickup he had bought off my uncle Pablo in Pleasanton and him and my mom came in a Volkswagen Gulf. They wanted to see where we lived and ended up staying in a hotel near the boardwalk in downtown Vallarta. When I got home I noticed my things where in the corner and I thought somebody had cleaned up and left them there.

Mauro and Martin who were friends of mine and also coworkers had said they weren't going to renew their contract when it expired on the 15th of May and I came back around the last week of April. They asked me if I was going to stay another month with Pablo, but I didn't know, so later that day I went to talk to him. Apparently, there was a misunderstanding about my stay with him. I thought he was charging me $1,000 pesos a month, but he was charging me that for three weeks while I look for a place.

I told Mauro about my situation and he said to stay with him, Martin and Arnold for the next week because he had decided to quit Mayan and go back to Guadalajara where he was going to be closer to his daughter. Martin and Arnold asked me if I wanted to go with them to Puerto Vallarta to live because they were tired of living in Valle Dorado, and to tell you the truth, I lived there for three weeks, and it was enough for me too. It's a town that wasn't engineered correctly. It doesn't have that many trees. It looks like a prison town, and in the rainy season, it floods so bad sometimes cars turn off when they pass because the water gets so high it's ridiculous.

Arnold Macias Torres on the edge of the cliff taken at Destiladera Beach in Nayarit. Now owned by Nahui Resorts. A public beach north of Nuevo Vallarta going towards Punta de Mita.

I had the Nissan pickup truck which gave us more freedom and the following weekend we didn't waste any more time and started exploring the beaches along the coastline. At first we decided to go to Punta de Mita which was north on the highway and into the Nayaritan Peninsula but ten minutes into the road we discovered Playa Destiladera. It was like arriving at a mini Cancun. The spot where we parked the car was at the end of a shallow cliff and you could see the aqua ocean on the horizon. It was an impeccable beach with miles of coastline, very clean, perfect for our taste. You could rent a table for a hundred pesos for the day or eat there and have the fee waived. We knew that with a grilled chicken and an 18-pack of Tecates the three of us could be there all day relaxing. I began to invest in beach supplies, the first thing was an umbrella and a chair, then an ice chest and so on. I already had the most important thing which was a vehicle to get there and the rest of my Sundays in Mexico would be like that whether somebody came with me or not.

Myself taking a break to pose for a picture at my cubicle in the reservations department of the contact center

In Mayan we worked one Saturday and the next one we had off, but since we were the rookies, I ended up working every Saturday for the next two months. In Mayan Resorts I had every single Sunday off but was required to work forty-eight hours a week unlike the US which was forty hours a week. In Mexico "overtime" doesn't exist if you end up working more or have to work more by your bosses demands you don't get paid more unless they're generous enough to do so which is hardly the case or in my case never and the minimum salary in Mexico is about 5 dikkars a day. Martin, Arnold and myself went to go see an apartment on the corner of Jamaica St. and Cuba St. two blocks east of the sports park near the downtown area in the Lazaro Cardenas neighborhood.

The apartment was the middle section of a three-story building in front of a church. The first floor was owned by a computer store and the upper floor was owned by our landlord's partners who were the owners of the whole building.. The apartment we ended up renting had three rooms, one small that looked like a walk in closet with a window overlooking the church, then the next room was a little bit bigger had two small balconies, one overlooking the church and the other one overlooking Cuba St., the third room was the biggest it actually had a closet and a big balcony overlooking Cuba St. and from there you could see the sports park.

The landlord was going to charge us $4,000.00 pesos a month ($333.00 dollars). The problem was all three of us wanted the big room but I didn't mind staying in the small room but I wasn't going to pay the same rent as the person staying in the big room and we all were on the same page about that. We broke it down as follows: the person in the small room is going to pay $1,100 pesos ($91.66 dollars) the middle room was $1,350 pesos ($112.50 dollars) and the big room is going to be $1550.00 pesos ($129.16 dollars). Martin ended up taking the big room, Arnold took over the medium room and I settled for the small room because I had the truck and had to pay for gasoline and insurance and really didn't need the big room. This way I saved some money.

From left to right: Arnold (Chino), myself and Martin at Club Roo in Puerto Vallarta. These guys would become an important role in adjusting my life in Vallarta becoming my roommates for a whole year.

The first day I had off to sleep in and wake up late was the first day I noticed what I hated about the location of the apartment. At exactly 6:00 A.M. every day the church next door sounded off the bells and it rang like there was no tomorrow, the only reason why I didn't notice it the other days was because I went to work by 5:45 A.M. and never heard the bells until the following Saturday I tried sleeping past 6:00 A.M. The first time was the worst of all because I didn't know. It was an equivalent of someone making the loudest sound out of anything right next to your ear while you're in a deep sleep. It looked like I was lost and confused. I ended up buying ear plugs and even with them I was able to hear the bells, but at least they sounded far away and not next to my ear.

Martin and Arnold told me they didn't notice the bells and laughed when I told them how pissed off I was every time they rang. As an atheist, I didn't care much for church, but every time the bells next door banged, it consumed my hatred more for religion with every passing moment I lived there.

I stopped going to Guadalajara by bus since I had the truck, but I started paying for gas and tolls on the federal roads. In Mexico there's two types of roads "libre" and "quota" which translates to "free roads" and "toll roads." The free roads are roads that take you through every little town there is and they usually zigzag a lot, but you pay no toll. The "toll roads" are roads constructed by the federal government which are heavily guarded by the military, but you pay a toll every so many kilometers.

For example if you go from Guadalajara to Puerto Vallarta they both take up the same time because the federal road kind of goes up towards Tepic, Nayarit and then at the end it curves down towards Vallarta whereas the free road goes through the mountain range and has a lot of curves. Both roads take about five hours to get from here to there but the federal road you're going to pay about $400 pesos ($37.50 dollars) in toll booths. At first I used to through the toll roads or federal roads because there was word going around the cartels would use the free roads a lot but after living in Mexico for a while I noticed the news hyped everything up more than it was.

I loved going to Guadalajara because my parents where there and I didn't have to think about work and it was a place of relaxation, but I came up with a conclusive decision, if I had to stay and live in Mexico for the rest of my life, it would be in Puerto Vallarta. After going to Guadalajara three or four times, I didn't like the big city ambience, the smog, the volume of people. Every time I would return home to Puerto Vallarta, even though I had to work six days a week for the majority of the time, the only day I had off was not only my day off it was like a vacation.

Punta Negra Beach fifteen minutes south of Old Vallarta on the coastal highway. You can see the Vallarta Resorts in the background.

I discovered another beach while I was living in Vallarta, which was the beach I would most visit during my stay called "Punta Negra." This beach was about fifteen minutes south of Vallarta taking the coastal highway towards the town of Barra de Navidad. I thought about the thousands of dollars everybody pays to get there like airflight, room accommodation and food while I lived twenty minutes from there, bought myself something to eat, twelve-pack of beers and I was good for the whole day. It was a good stress-free environment that made me wake up the next day and go to work happily. Martin, Arnold (by that time we called him "Chino" Chinese in

Spanish) and myself had our own routine going on since we worked at different times. I had the 7:00 A.M. to 4:00 P.M. schedule, and when I got home every day, I ate quesadillas. I never was a good cook or knew how to prepare meals efficiently in the kitchen. I would buy $20 pesos ($1.60 dollars) worth of cheese, 300 grams of meat, a packet of twelve tortillas, an onion and two tomatoes, that would last me two dinners which would amount roughly about $60 pesos ($5 dollars). We got our paycheck every two weeks and there were times were I only had a few bucks in my pocket and payday was still a few days away so I would open a couple of cans of tuna and that was my dinner.

My daily routine would be to get home after work eat some quesadillas, read a little bit, go to the gym and by the time I would get back Chino and Martin would already be there and then we would go to the sports park to play soccer or run laps. On the weekends we would all do our own thing and by now you know that my thing was… the beach.

LEFT: My mom making us some home-made food and eating it on the balcony of our apartment form left to right: Maria holding Alyssa, Alicia (mom), Martin (white shirt), Chino (gray tank top)

RIGHT: My dad walking Alyssa across the street. Our apartment is the middle section of the white building.

After a few months passed by and my parents decided to visit me in my new place and to my luck a day before they arrived the water was cut off all because the neighbors upstairs and downstairs had a disagreement between the water bill and we were literally stuck in the middle of everything, even though we were paying our bills. When I gave my landlord a call, he told me everybody in the neighborhood had the water cut off by accident, but when I looked out the window, I saw the neighbors washing the sidewalk with their hose. I left him an unpleasant voicemail stating if he's not going to do anything, I was going to go to the city and see how they can resolve this problem. He called back and told me he was going to bring containers with water to the house while he figures out how to get the water back. He came in his truck with eight containers that held about five gallons each full of water.

My parents over all had a good time with the only inconvenience of having to bathe with buckets of water versus the shower head. I learned with that experience I was able to take a shower with only a 5 gallon bucket of water versus in the United States we take water for granted and most of the time waste it unnecessarily. In the winter months where it was a little bit cooler and sometimes we ran out of gas, we had to shower with cold water and learned warm and hot water were a luxury. Try taking a shower with cold water in the winter months in the early morning when you wake up and then say that you're not having a good day because your phone didn't charge or your local Starbucks didn't have whip cream when you went through.

I would see my daughter grow up through the phone at first since we didn't have internet. I missed my wife and daughter too much and got desperate, so I told her to come and live in Vallarta while the immigration case settled. My friend Martin Galindo from back home in the Bay Area who also had his own company Galindo's Drywall did me a favor by looking for a trustworthy person to rent our house while Maria and Alyssa came with me.

One of his friends Rigoberto and his wife Raquel did the favor of moving in so we didn't lose our house in Oakley, California to foreclosure. I told him just to clear the mortgage payments without charging him anything extra or deposit until I get back. It was a two-story, two-bedroom with a nook, two and a half bathrooms, one of the rooms was full of our stuff along with the garage, they had access to about 85 percent of the house and that's the way it was until the day I was to come back.

My parents with Alyssa visiting us from Guadalajara. We're in front of Mangos club and restaurant next to the Vallarta Boardwalk.

After a while of living in Mexico I noticed the way of life was more re-laxing than in the States. In the United States the only news they receive of Mexico is bad news like any news organization telling us about the worst of the world. In Mexico the same biased news happened, the image about living in the states was horrifying letting its citizens the right to buy guns with simply a background check. Almost every news that came from the States was a shooting at a school or a mall or somewhere where people where ter-rorized by a lunatic.

Everybody I knew never wanted to visit the US because they thought they were going to get shot or killed in a public area. The time I lived in Mexico you can say that it was the best time of my life. I really felt what it was like to be stress free without frustration or being part of a system where they're always out to get you. I didn't have to worry about the government spying on me or breaking the abundant amounts of rules and laws created that make you func-tion almost like a utopian society against your nature to express yourself with-out breaking the law.

This picture taken by my wife Maria is a symbol representing Mexican freedom where in the United States it would be considered "child endangerment" in Mexico you have certain liberties that make life stress free. Whenever my daughter would go back to the United States she would hate being thrown in the back of the car without a panoramic view.

In the United States they brainwash you on a daily basis through propaganda about the civil liberties implemented and through a powerful military keeping everybody safe, but in reality, until you experience real freedom, the only freedom in the United States is the freedom to make yourself believe you're free. One way of living I do have to give credit were credit is due is in the United States the fact you are able to save money because the way of life is cheaper in a materialistic sense. In the United States you make dollars and spend dollars; in Mexico you make pesos and spend in dollars.

When we got deported and started to buy stuff for the first time, I thought to myself "well, at least we're in Mexico now and since everything is in pesos it's going to be cheaper." Up until this day the only thing I saw in Mexico cheaper than the United States was domestic beer, tacos from your local eatery (excluding tourist zones). Rent because the houses are smaller than your typical two- or three-bedroom house in the States and labor. If you buy clothes, a car, a computer, or take yoga classes or buy a DVD at your local store, it's going to cost you the same or more expensive in Mexico. A friend of my dad's once told him "the United States is a practical society whereas in Mexico we are an aesthetic society." I asked my dad what it meant and his answer made me understand a little bit more on where we as a culture come from.

In the United States you buy a pair of shoes because they're comfortable because they're going to do the job you want them to do like run or walk in Mexico we buy shoes because it says "Nike" or "Vans" not because they're comfortable, Mexico is a nation of brands and we don't care if we spend half of our check on a pair of shoes or a brand-name shirt. We'd rather eat $5 peso tacos from down the corner, but when it comes to the latest trend, we're not going to be behind at all.

I went to Juarez for the first time the last week of September 2011 and had mentally prepared for a physical exam and an interview made by the US Consulate which Maria and our lawyer Marcia had prepared. My mom told me my aunt Eva had sent me $800 dollars to help me with whatever I needed for the trip and to this day I am grateful for her gesture. At my job the only thing they were concerned was if I was going to be there on opening day which was the first of every month.

The general manager of my company was very sympathetic to my case probably because he was an immigrant himself being English living in Mexico. Maria bought me the Juarez ticket through Vivaerobus.com with a layover in Monterey via Guadalajara. I left Vallarta on September 23rd 2011 arriving in Guadalajara five hours later at the bus station in Zapopan where my parents were waiting. I had clothes for a couple of days and a 300-page packet my lawyer had prepared for the interview. The packet was a pardon set forth to cancel the ten-year ban I had been given after being deported to Mexico, you are susceptible to get it as soon as you get thrown across the border thanks to the immigration policies of the Bill Clinton administration back in the '90s.

I arrived in Juarez on September 26 at night and I was somewhat nervous because I was suddenly in a border town where more than half of the bad news came from. As soon as you came off from the plane and picked up your baggage you would pay for a taxi inside the airport before you stepped outside. You would either go to zone 1 or zone 2. I was going to zone 1 and had to pay $245.00 pesos ($18.85 dollars) for them to take me there.

Before you travel anywhere, it's always good to research the place and what to expect, so I read about something called "casa de huespedes" which translates to "guest houses." It's people renting out rooms for people coming out of town giving them a cheaper price than a hotel or motel and they usually give taxi drivers a commission to bring them there and that's exactly what my taxi driver did as we started to leave the airport. I already had everything purchased via internet, so I told him to drive me to the Microtel Inn Suites that was right next door to the US emabassy.

On Tuesday the 27th, I went to take the physical exam required for the interview. I got there around 7:00 A.M. and left around 3:00 P.M. It was more waiting around than anything else. The building is located next to the Microtel Inn right next to the consulate, right in the middle. The first window is to give your stack of papers along with your passport; then you go through a glass door and wait to get blood drawn. The next test is an eye exam like when you to the DMV only it's a lady dressed in white with latex gloves administering it. The next step was a very uncomfortable one where you had to pee in a cup while a male nurse looked at your crotch to make sure you don't cheat. The second to last step is a place where they tell you to go into a small room and you have to get naked and the doctor touches your chest plate, stomach goes down and touches your testicles and asks you if you have tattoos or scars.

They take pictures of your scars or tattoos. In my case I had the fifth sun from the Aztec calendar and on my right arm I had the "Hecho en Mexico" emblem. They ask you if you had done drugs before and I told him when I was about fifteen years old I smoked Marijuana, and he writes all the information in his book. He then asked me when was the last time I did it and replied there was a cookie incident that happened to me a year ago where somebody laced it with marijuana, but before I could continue with my explanation, he said that was enough wrote it down and told me to step outside on the hallway.

While you're waiting in the hallway you only have your pants on, and then they put you in a room where they take an x-ray of your chest plate. The last step is all the vaccines you have to get, and in my case, there were three on my right arm and the other two on my left arm. The total was $350 dollars. You can pay in dollars or pesos and after you go to the cashier's window, they give you back your passport they let you know you can pick up your results the following day.

Before you leave you step into a psychologist office so you can talk about the physical exam, the only concern she was interested in was the fact that I had previously smoked marijuana and I gave her a random number which was five 'cause I didn't really care how much I had smoked it before. After about seven to ten minutes, she made me sign a paper and let me go. I went back to the hotel to rest then hit the gym a little bit, and at the end of the day, I spoke with Maria via SKYPE.

The following day I was at the consulate for my interview and mentally prepared myself for another day of just waiting around. When you enter the compound it's like entering an airport, there are metal detectors and you give them your appointment paper, and they give you back a number that's going to be your reference to go to your interviewer. You go through the back of the security building and they have a section with a lot of bleachers sitting in front of about five to six big screen TV's hanging with all the numbers of the people waiting to be interviewed.

When your number comes up, you go up to the window it shows next to your number. There's a section inside the building but reserved only for the elderly, pregnant women, or women who had to bring their kids with them. I must've waited about three to four hours before my number came up. When it did, I walked up to the window it had showed me to go to and the guy who was to be my interviewer was your typical Caucasian arrogant prick who thought he was better than anybody there.

A real asshole, he kind of looked like an anorexic comedian Andy Dick with a perm. Every question he gave me was to pinch my last nerve or to get some kind of rise out of me, but I maintained my cool and did everything I could do to take in all the bullshit I was about to receive. He asked me when was my first time I came into the United States I said 1986 and the paper said 1987 and he was telling me that I was a liar, I told him I was six or seven years old, and I didn't remember exactly but everything was in the paper he was looking at. He asked me where was I raised and when I said California he quickly responded while rolling his eyes back "oh LA of course" already profiling me with his tone of voice and then I responded back "the San Francisco Bay Area."

He then asked me to tell him about the tattoos I had. I told him they represented my culture and to keep pissing me off he told me if I knew the tattoos I had where gang related to which I said no. He gave me a sheet with another appointment set for October 3 which was in four days and to immediately exit the consulate with a condescending tone. They kept my passport, but luckily, I had my IFE if I needed to fly back. I called my work and let them know what was going on, but my supervisor was being a dick and said I couldn't take the extra days off because they were waiting for me for opening day.

I talked to my dad, and he told me to come home to Guadalajara and while Maria and Alyssa stayed at my parents, I would go back to work for opening day and come back on Sunday to head back to Juarez again. To sum up this fiasco, I took a plane back to Guadalajara on Thursday night, drove Friday morning to Vallarta, went to work on Saturday at Mayan Resorts, stayed there Saturday and when I woke up on Sunday drove back to Guadalajara and jumped on a plane to Juarez to get ready for my secondary review on Monday morning.

I got a little mad at my supervisor because most of the time he was on a power trip. He's your typical "I'm your supervisor and it's going to go the way I say" kind of person and instead of helping you, they don't care. They love abusing their power over you. We didn't really have a lot of calls, and he could've saved me some money, but I was there letting him know I wasn't going to bitch about it, though he could've handled it differently. I could've left to Guadalajara right after work, but to destress myself I went out and left the next day.

This time when I went to Juarez, I stayed at the Krystal Business hotel and while it was farther down from the consulate, it was a nicer hotel and had complimentary shuttle service to the consulate. The same process to go into the consulate and the waiting period began. This time when they called me, I was waiting outside a small interrogation room along with two other guys who, by looking at these guys, they looked like your local gang members waiting for trial and as soon as they saw me they were puzzled as to why they were there so both of them asked me if I had tattoos and suddenly it hit me: they were going to ask us about our tattoos and the reason for them.

I was the last of the three to go in, and the guy interviewing us looked like a detective from the TV show *Law & Order* with his badge on the front of his belt so you could see it and a black goatee that made him look like Robert de Niro from the movie *Heat*. When he interviewed me, he was more laidback than the first prick—the Andy Dick look-alike. He asked me about the marijuana and I told him I was trying to explain to the doctor about the cookie incident where it was laced and all, but it seemed the doctor didn't care and was more receptive and understanding.

He then went on to see if during my time in California I had ever experienced danger through any kind of gang activity towards me because of the tattoos I carry to which I responded "on the contrary I get plenty of positive comments." After about ten or fifteen minutes, he then sent me to go outside to sit back and wait for them to call my name again.

Another two hours passed by and they called me to another window with another interviewer. This guy looked like the men's warehouse role model with a nice suit he just cleaned and he kind of sounded like a rookie but was very professional in the way he talked to me. He asked me to briefly tell him what had happened and when I got to the date of my deportation. He then shocked me with the next question, but I don't know if this is part of a trick they do on people or he really didn't know what the hell was going on, but he asked me how come after my deportation on October 27, 2010 I tried to illegally go back into the United States.

At first, I thought he was looking at somebody else's file. but it seemed he was pretty serious, I answered back after they dropped us off at the border by Tijuana, I never came back by any means. We spent two days in Tijuana, then after October 29, we were in Guadalajara. He then gave me three different dates that ICE had captured me crossing illegally in November, and I was puzzled and before I could ask him if he was looking at my file. He turned off the microphone and went to go ask some guy in the back a question about something on the screen he was looking at and they both came over to the window.

I couldn't tell what they were talking about because he still had the microphone off, but I could hear their voice a little bit through the plexiglass window and my interviewer was telling the other agent my story didn't match the story on his screen. I don't know what the other guy said, but after a couple of minutes, he turned on the microphone back and told me I qualify for a pardon, and they were going to let me know via DHL ground transport to the destination picked by my lawyer in a couple of weeks. Later Marcia told me they play tricks like that on people at the interview to catch them in a lie automatically assuming we're all dishonest.

After a couple of weeks, I received a letter via DHL in Guadalajara with my passport and we got excited, but as Maria started reading the letter, they said they didn't find sufficient information to allow the pardon and my case was going to be sent to secondary review. I got upset and lost my hope completely, so I began to realize I was going to stay in Mexico and then began thinking why am I spending all this money in pardons and going to Juarez when I could be spending it more intelligently in Mexico. When I got back to Vallarta, I started to find out information about buying a house and mentally prepared myself I was going to live there for the rest of my life.

My father and daughter overlooking the beach at Barra de Navidad where my dad grew up as a kid.

When I turned a year at Mayan resorts on February 1, 2012, I decided to use my week vacation and leave to Guadalajara. My parents had wanted to take a trip to Barra de Navidad ever since we got there because its where my parents used to go a lot in their younger years. My dad used to go for months at a time with his brother Oscar and his cousin Kiko. We left and after three hours and four toll booths later, we arrived in Colima The panoramic views are awesome including the Nevado and Colima Volcanoes. We stayed in a hotel near the downtown area and my dad showed us where he ran around when he was a kid living there. After we ate breakfast at a local eatery, we went to visit his uncle at la Dulceria Reyes from his mom's side of the family it was a candy shop dating back about fifty years or so.

Picture taken by my dad at the Colima downtown area. From left to right, my mom with Alyssa in the stroller, my wife Maria and myself.

While we headed back to the hotel through downtown my mom and Maria went in to the local shops to look around my dad spotted a guy on the corner selling "tuba." The "tuba" is a very delicious drink made from the palm tree leaf. If you wanted fresh, you have to buy it early in the morning because it starts going bad real fast and the "tuba" sellers start adding sugar or other preservatives to keep it fresh. We got back into the car and headed towards the city of Tecoman where my dad wanted to visit his uncle Jorge Messina.

I was excited to meet somebody related to us I had never met before, and when we got to Tecoman, my mom asked my dad if he remembered where he lived. My dad said he didn't remember, but it shouldn't be hard because and his exact words where "everybody knows the Messina's out here" and apparently my great uncle used to be a very important person there. He was even mayor of Tecoman back in 1985. Now the million-dollar question is are we just going to go up to a random residence or business and ask for Jorge Messina? My dad said, "Why not?"

My mother and I thought it was the most ridiculous idea ever, but after arriving at the downtown area, my dad stopped the car, saw a mechanic shop, got out of the car and went to ask them. My mom and I looked at each other like saying, let him go ask, and then we'll be on our way to the next destination. When my dad came back, he said "told you so, my uncle lives about seven blocks from here to the right." I almost wanted to believe it, but I needed to see his house with him in it first. We got to a house on the corner of a street and as we were getting out there was two people sitting on the porch and one of them was an old man with gray hair and a pair of glasses to which I heard him say "those people right there look like Messina's" and my dad responded with "hi, Uncle!" I couldn't believe some random person in the street knew my great uncle. We went in through the front gate and on the front yard they had banana, orange, and lemon trees growing everywhere.

We stepped up to the porch to say hi and when my great uncle Jorge got up he must've been at least six foot four, and for a seventy-eight-year-old man, that was impressive knowing I'm related to this person made me feel proud of where my family came from. We were there for about forty-five minutes to chit chat and left. We passed by Manzanillo, which looked a lot like Oakland back home; it's a big port city where cargo ships come from the states and the orient. We arrived at Barra de Navidad that's right next to Melaque. both beach towns.

We stayed in Barra de Navidad a night, but my dad was kind of disappointed. It wasn't like he remembered. I mean after twenty years, what did you expect? Besides after living in Vallarta where the city is investing on infrastructure and the private sector is investing in its entertainment industry, it's like going to Reno after you've been so many times to Vegas. Even though we were kind of let down by how Barra looked, I was glad to be able to have had a trip like that with my parents because they hadn't taken any time to actually go out and relax since the deportation, and they hadn't gone to Barra since more than twenty years ago.

Picture taken by me. My brother Ruber is in the ocean swimming and you can't really see him, only a little black dot which is his head at the center right. He couldn't believe how warm the ocean gets in August and thought of it as a "natural jacuzzi."

Summer in Vallarta is intense and it rains like there is no tomorrow and to control the mosquito population industrial trucks pass by the neighborhoods spraying a gas like substance into the air. You can tell when people are out of town like from Guadalajara or Mexico City because they blast the AC. My roommates Martin and Chino bought themselves fans to survive the coastal heat. I didn't mind sleeping and waking up in a pool of sweat I enjoyed the inferno like climate. Mayan Resorts is a place where you work for a short period of time but not really a place where you can make a career. By working there, it helped me see what it's like to work hard and then feel like nobody value the work you do. On the other hand, all the people I worked with in the department helped each other there and outside and we became like a brotherhood of the contact center. Since I was the only one with a truck, I helped a lot of people move.

By this time, I had all the knowledge on how to buy a house in Mexico and decided to go for it with my parents' blessing. In Mexico there's a government program called Infonavit and through infonavit there is a point system made to help you buy a house. It was May of 2012 and according to Infonavit my points would be eligible until November of 2013 and who knows what was going to happen by that time.

I told them if there was any other way, I could buy a house like putting a certain percentage towards the capital. They gave me an option through a new program called "sure credit" where depending on your age and the time you've invested in the company you're working for and your salary, you would put a down payment on an account, there would be a four-month grace period, then you would get the certificate and give it to the realty company to process your mortgage.

My numbers came through after I gave them all the information and told me I had to have $60,000.00 pesos ($5,000.00 dollars) on an account in Bansefi. I started the process on May 3, 2012 which meant by September 3, I would get the green light for my house. We went to a new track of homes located behind the convention center and Galerias mall Vallarta it was called Villas de Paraiso in the neighborhood of Club Paseo del Hipodromo. Jose Navarro was the agent who helped and guided me through the purchase of my first home.

The house was worth $416,000.00 pesos ($34,666.00 dollars) and to my luck when we started signing for the loan, they dropped to $378,000.00 pesos ($31,500 dollars). When he told me about the news, I had already been approved for the property value that was worth more so instead of getting the cheapest one on the first floor, I got the one on the second floor and on the corner.

I had to go to Juarez again in October 2012 after opening day which was the first of every month. I had to do the physical exam again because it expires after one year. My lawyer, Marcia was already on top of it and gave my wife the papers needed for me to bring. I began again the journey to Juarez driving to Guadalajara October 2nd 2012 but this time I wasn't excited to go at all. I left Guadalajara airport and arrived in Juarez on October 3 and stayed at the Mircotel Inn Suites. When I did the medical exam, it was the same process as last time; the only difference is it went faster because there were only about twenty people in the whole building getting it done.

The only thing I wasn't expecting is when I got to the psychologist's office, she asked me to tell her exactly how many times I inhaled marijuana and the number had to match the number I gave her the first time and it's the number written on the report she was holding from a year ago. I honestly didn't remember what number I gave her, so I told her about two or three times. She told me if I wanted to step outside and come back in because there were people that were taking this seriously.

I lost my patience and told her it didn't matter how many times I went out and back in, I wasn't going to remember. She then told me they had previously denied status to liars like me and I told her my priority was to get back to my family in the States not to remember some number I gave them about how many times I did pot.

I left disappointed, upset and frustrated and couldn't believe this arrogant prick of a person who, her being Mexican, instead of helping me would be the cause of the US government denying my VISA. I left and went to the consulate, but they told me I didn't have an appointment. I went back to the hotel room and called Maria who then called Marcia. Maria had told me Marcia made the appointment via internet and it was scheduled for the next day of my physical exam but the guards at the consulate told me I didn't have one. The results of my exam were to be delivered through DHL to the consulate and I would have my answer in two weeks. I decided to take a taxi to the nearest DHL drop off location and send in the results before I leave to Guadalajara, I figured it be cheaper and faster.

When I got back to Vallarta hopeless, I channeled my negativity into a positive train of thought and concentrated in getting my house and starting my life over by taking a step forward. I had completely forgotten they were going to have an answer for me in two weeks and out of the blue my dad sends me a text I received a package that he picked up. Only myself or my lawyer could pick up the package, but I had left my dad a copy of my identification and a power of attorney letter stating he could pick anything up in my absence.

The text he sent me was very blunt and mundane that read "you got a package from the consulate, check your email." Since he didn't tell me anything else on the text, I assumed it wasn't good news or I had to go back to Juarez. I was ready to throw in the towel. I wasn't going back to Juarez. They could take their precious green card system and shove it up their ass. At this point I was done throwing away my money and wasting my time playing by their game. I told my dad I would check it later.

When I got home, I checked my email my dad had sent me with an attachment. He scanned everything and sent it so I could see exactly what they had sent. It was my passport, but the only different thing in it was the stamp by the federal government granting me access back to the United States. I couldn't believe it, two years I had been waiting for news like this, I was ready to give the whole process the middle finger, what if I had to go one more time for them to give me the green light? I sent my dad a text immediately giving him a thank-you for picking it up, and he congratulated me.

I sent Maria a message because by this time she had gone back to the States to live and asked her to let my lawyer Marcia know I wasn't ready to go back right away and to let me know if there is a deadline on when I had to go back by. Maria later told me as soon as she let our lawyer know I wasn't going to come back right way she was surprised and why not? After all the time and money spent I wouldn't go back right away.

My explanation to her via email was because it's not that I didn't want to go back, it's just that I had some things I couldn't leave undone like the house I just purchased they hadn't even given me the keys to it, and also I didn't want to do what ICE did to us where they just throw us over the border without the chance of saying goodbye to anybody. I had a life and friends now I couldn't just pick up and go again. I had to prepare myself about all the obstacles awaiting my return to the "land of opportunity."

Marcia told me I had until April 1, 2013 to go back, and if I didn't everything we did would be lost and have to do the process over again and it's not the same being a VISA account holder and being a permanent resident if the laws changed in another direction they could take my VISA away but by coming back to the states as soon as I land, I would be a permanent resident and I would be safe. I began to let the couple letting me rent their apartment about my situation and where I would be headed by the end of the year. David and Hortencia were the nicest landlords I ever came across. I gave them our information in case they ever wanted to come to the Bay Area.

When I decided on a date to go back to California, which was around mid-January I started telling my circle of friends I was going to leave Mayan Resorts soon. One of them was Sharon Rojas. While I was in Vallarta, she rented a business studio in the Marina where she had different instructors teach a trade, and in my case, I taught self-defense and circuit training. I owe a lot to her;

even at work she always had my back or if I needed a lift somewhere she was there. The knowledge I gained from my sensei Bright at the Oakley American Karate Academy paid off, even though I didn't completely finish black belt the experience helped me a lot.

On my birthday, Sharon and Mara took me out for drinks at the Sonora Prime Grill in the Marina and it's where I told them I was leaving because Sharon wanted to renew her contract for the studio. I didn't want to leave her hanging or make her think I wasn't going to be there. I made them promise not to tell anyone because I wasn't ready. Our last day of classes was November 30, 2012. She told me she wishes I wasn't leaving because she values my friendship and never let her down with the studio classes but understood I was doing this for my family.

My house in Puerto Vallarta, mine is the second story corner apartment. You go up the stairs and make a left all the way down. The gray Nissan pickup truck I drove for a year and a half while I was in Vallarta is parked.

The first week of November the agency that I bought the house from told me of an appointment at the Infonavit building at Caracol Plaza which took a couple of hours. Since my loan was a little different. Instead of the usual fifteen-day grace period, it would take thirty days, which I calculated around mid-December. In the meeting they told all of us who were there to sign papers, and I still remember to this day "as of today you are all homeowners." Wow, I couldn't believe what I was hearing. All those years living in the United States I could never own anything. I mean I had a house and cars but nothing ever to my name until that day. It was like when you get a new toy and you know it's yours and nothing is going to happen to it as long as you take care of it. I almost put in my two weeks' notice at my job on December 8 so I could spend Christmas in Guadalajara with my parents but I know I was going to need a little seed money to start furnishing my new house.

After the first week of December passed and I didn't get notification about getting the keys to my house, my friend Sharon told me to get at it because in Mexico they usually close off government offices in mid-December and don't open up until mid-January. I called them the second week of December and set up a date for me to go pick up the keys which ended up being on 12/12/12. I texted my dad to let him know we had a place in Vallarta, and he told me he also had some good news he wanted to share but not through the phone, and even though I implored him to tell me he wanted to do it in person.

I spent Christmas with my parents in Guadalajara and on December 21, 2012, I hit the road thinking to myself this was the date the world was supposedly going to end according to the Aztec calendar. Well, if it does end at least I'm going from one side of paradise to the other. At work since the 25th and the 1st were national holidays, we didn't work them but they landed on a Tuesday, which meant half of the contact center was to work on the 24th and the other half was to work on the 30th. I didn't care about working the 30th because I was planning to spend New Year's in Vallarta, but I wanted to spend Christmas in Guadalajara.

Unfortunately, it ended up being backwards, and since I was already planning to quit anyways, I decided to take the 24th and risk being written-up because to me it didn't matter anyway and to my luck when I came back nobody in management knew I was going because of the small volume of calls handled on the 24th.

At the dinner table on the 25th after my mom served us a delicious dinner, we were all in our little world having conversations with each other (two brothers, my parents and I) my dad asked to have a word and we all turned to him in silence, then he says he's going to give us his Christmas present and turns to me and says "Remember I wanted to tell you something, but I wanted to wait for the right moment?" I said yea. "They made me quit my job today and asked for my resignation."

If at that moment you would've looked around the table we all had the same face of "what the hell kind of good news is that?!" I began to think things like *this was your Christmas present that you were fired? Did I miss something? A gift card would've been better.* Then before my mind kept wondering more into the unknown, I stopped and kept listening while my dad continued. "The reason I quit is because they promoted me to President of the COBAEJ." It's a University in Guadalajara, and he was going to be in charge along with twenty other presidents in the whole state of Jalisco.

We were dumbfounded and excited at the same time and any negative thoughts we had from the beginning of the conversation vanished without a trace. It was an ending to a very good year for the Messina family despite everything that had happened. My brother Jonathan who lived in Vallarta with me told us they offered him a supervisor position in the company he was working for called "el nogalito," which does zipline tours for tourists. In less than two years our family was able to stand up strong against that autumn morning in October of 2010.

All my friends came and joined in my last gathering at the beach in the Bucerias, Nayarit downtown area right next to restaurant "el gordo's."

I had told my friends I wanted a farewell party by the beach the last Saturday I was to spend in Vallarta and on January 19. All of my closest of friends came through to the Bucerias beach right next to "el gordo" restaurant to have a good time. My friend Jimmy had a friend who had a small establishment there was gracious enough to let us plug Jimmy's equipment so we can listen to music. Coincidentally the patron festivities of Bucerias where going on and if you wanted some tacos, pizza, hot dogs, or basically any kind of food for the munchies it was there until late into the night. One of the many good things about the freedom in Mexico is when you have a party like that in the open you never have to worry about the cops or anybody calling the cops. It's not like the United States where you can't make any noise after 10:00 P.M. or they'll cite you for noise pollution.

My friend Martin would also quit Mayan and decided to move to Guadalajara and asked me to wait for him and help him out with his things because I was leaving most of my stuff at my new place.

By this time, I was done furnishing my place I did everything from painting it to buying all the furniture and leaving it ready for vacation purposes. The only two things I wasn't able to do because of time was buy a mattress for Alyssa's room and put air conditioning but other than that, it was ready. We hit the road and left Guadalajara on January 26, 2012 through the free roads going through Mascota and its Esmeralda Sierra.

We stopped to eat in Mascota and ate the most delicious grilled fish with some cold beer. The restaurant we stopped at is next to a reservoir and is owned by the De Santiago Dueñas family, and they do extraordinary work in making sure your dining experience is the best. We kept going towards Guadalajara and arrived in the evening at where Martin would stay. I helped him unload his stuff and headed to my parents' place where they were waiting for me to arrive. My parents and brothers waited for me to go out to eat, and Chino got there a little bit after to join us in my final meal.

We went to a restaurant in the Tapatio Plaza which is a five-minute walk from my parents' place and ate there. Afterwards my parents and my brothers were tired, and even though I was also tired from the road and the dinner, Martin, Chino, and I decided to keep the party going by heading to Chapultepec Avenue where all the clubs and bars happen to congregate. We started at a bar with some shots and ended up bar hopping our way through the avenue. At the last bar we went to we ordered fifteen beers for like $14 dollars, which was ridiculously cheap and everybody around us looked at us like we were crazy.

As that was happening, my friend Martin goes "that's right, bitch, we don't order one we order fifteen at a time." We couldn't even finish the last of the beers so we asked for a to-go cup and they gave us a big foam cup so we could fit two or three beers at a time. I left Chino with his friends on the corner of Manuel Doblado and Javier Mina and Martin and I headed back to my folks' pad to crash.

On Sunday my dad and I took Martin back to where he was going to stay and we said our goodbyes. My parents and I went to Tequila to show me where he had bought two pieces of land. The land was on the outside of Tequila officially in Magdalena, which is the town next door to Tequila. When you're arriving, it looks like when you're entering a forest. It's in the hills, and they've made it so you're in the middle of nature with trees and boulders everywhere. There were wooden stakes in the ground to let you know which property was yours. We probably stayed there for about forty minutes, taking pictures and scoping out the place. We stopped at a small place to eat and tasted a spicy hot sauce made from peanuts that was very good.

We didn't stay long in Tequila and left to Guadalajara because my uncle Oscar and his family were waiting for us to bid me a farewell and had a cake made for me that read "good trip."

The next day on Tuesday the 29th (my last day) my mother and I decided to spend some time where she likes it best...in the streets shopping. I bought some last-minute things for Maria and my daughter. I bought Maria some earrings from the jewelry building at the Tapatia Plaza and since Alyssa loves Mickey Mouse. I got her a Minnie Mouse doll and my son Joel some toys like a kite and a water gun. My mom did my suitcase because if I would've done it, it would've exploded when I opened it up back home.

While my mom packed, my dad and I sat at the table and he helped me remember some pointers on how he ran Messina's Landscaping. We revised strategies and came up with mnemonic devices to help me remember key objectives. He ran Messina's Landscaping for more than seven years, but really his knowledge of the trade began way before. I knew how to do the labor part of the job, but my dad did the customer service part of it. He naturally exceeded at his oratorical skills. I took notes like if I was going to take a final exam the next day and carry them with me to this day in my head. This was to be my career as soon as I was to start work when I got to California.

My parents took me to the airport it still didn't hit me I was going back to the States by plane and mostly because of all the trips I had to take to Juarez during the past two years it felt somewhat normal. We went to the airport's Burger King and sat down for an hour and a half until it was time for me to board. As soon as we were saying our goodbyes, after I gave my dad a big hug and a kiss, I turned to my mom and did the same thing but noticed her eyes where watery and reddish.

I knew right there and then I wasn't going to be able to see them in some time and a nostalgic wave of feelings started to take over me. An indescribable emotion knowing they weren't four hours away by car anymore, but three and a half by plane.

As I left them at the terminal and started to walk away I quietly and slowly started breaking down, I kept walking as if nothing was wrong, but tears started rolling down my cheeks as if there was a broken water main in the corner of my eye. I couldn't stop it even when I really tried and thought about something else it just kept coming, so I let it be until my body was able to naturally calm down. I felt guilty about leaving the only two people in the world who ever had my back unconditionally even, and for the first time, I was going to be very far from them.

I passed through all the security checkpoints, then sat close to where my airline was. I had my notebook computer with me and opened it up to look at some pictures and noticed there was a free Wi-Fi connection available at my discretion. To lighten up my mood I decided to prank my wife Maria. I saw she was on SKYPE and called her hoping she would pick up. She had just gotten home from the gym and was about to start getting ready to pick me up later. I told her there was a problem with my VISA and I wasn't going to be able to arrive that night. It didn't even last three seconds when she started to get hyped up and asking me in a firm tone of voice what kind of problem there was. I couldn't continue with it so I told her it was a joke and ended up both of us laughing it off.

Volaris flight #970 ascended from Guadalajara at 20:00 hours central standard time on January 29 and landed in Sacramento, California at 21:50 P.M. PST. The flight was exactly like the ocean that came with me that night very "pacific." I didn't have a watch or any device to tell time, so I asked the youngster next to me for the time so I could input it on my mp3. In Mexico the only time where I would wear shoes was to go to work or to exercise, otherwise because of the warm weather, I was always in sandals, but this time as I headed towards the United States, I kept my shoes on knowing when I stepped outside the plane the weather was going to be the same as my mood very cold and unpleasant. When I left Guadalajara it was about 26 degrees Celsius (80 Farenheit) I arrived at Sacramento, California where it was 5 degrees Celsius (40 Farenheit).

When I got out of the plane and felt the cold refrigerator air compromising the integrity of my skin, I completely had forgotten how cold it could get and how useful or better yet important mittens, socks, and possibly a scarf, if I had one, was. I never had been through US Customs before as an adult, by myself AND coming from Mexico as a Mexican. I followed what everybody was doing and saw the people going over to some counter and grabbing a form to declare what were you bringing into the country, the amount of money you had, and if there was any fruits or vegetables.

Then instead of having more booths open there was only two or three working for about two hundred people that just came off an airplane. I had previously told Maria not to arrive early because it takes about an hour to go through customs and worse yet they had told me I was going to get processed since I'm a "new immigrant." When it was my turn to go up to the customs agent, I gave him my passport and then he asked for my green card. I told him I had some papers I was supposed to give him and he asked to see what I had.

As I was getting the necessary documents from my carry-on he opened my passport and when he saw the seal of the United States, he said, "Oh you're a new immigrant, it takes me a while to process new immigrants so have a seat." There were some chairs across from his booth up against the wall, and he told me if I had any suitcases to go and get them and come back to wait until he called me up.

All the passengers had gone through, and then he called me up and started the process. He asked me to take off my white panama jack hat I had on for him to take a picture, this hat was the only tangible memory I had from Vallarta. He took the fingerprint from my right index finger and then I signed a blank federal document Homeland Security would later fill out. He asked me some routine questions about how I got my VISA and so forth, so I told him a little bit about my deportation and what my future plans were. It felt more like a conversation between two ordinary people than an interview between a new immigrant and an officer of the law. He stamped my passport and told me my green card would arrive at the address it was put on the original petition, which was in Galt, California where my in-laws lived.

I asked him the only question that was floating through my mind at the time which was "do I have to wait until I get my green card to go visit my parents in Mexico?" he responded with "With this stamp you can come and go whenever you want; you can go tomorrow if you like." I couldn't believe he just told me I could come and go, I thanked him, and he wished me good luck and off I went.

As I was leaving that section of the airport there were two airport agents asking me if I had wooden things or food in my bags, which I didn't and then the next room through the glass doors I had to put my bags again and then take an airtrain to baggage claim which was really weird. As I was walking downstairs to baggage claim I saw my wife Maria and her brother Mark entering like if we planned my pickup precisely to the second.

We picked up my bags and left the airport, I suddenly started to have withdrawals about Mexico and because I hadn't eaten since the early afternoon, they took me to a drive-in selling tacos and quesadillas in Elk Grove. They tasted like crap, but it took my hunger away to say the least. It felt surreal being back, almost as if I was dreaming. It was hard to come back after the government yanked my family and myself from a life we had already molded with family and friends two years, three months, and two days ago.

January 29 is one of those many dates recorded in the back of my mind because it ended a very small part of my life that became very significant in a very small amount of time and because I was thrown back into the mix to continue the American dream for my family without them. My daughter was very shy around me. I gave her the Minnie Mouse I bought her, and she grabbed it and ran behind my wife. She was still shy around me, but it was understandable being absent for more than six months.

Mark took me to the DMV around 2:00 P.M. to take the DMV exam for my driver's license. I took the eye and written exam and since I had an expired driver's license from Wisconsin the driving test was waived. Mark had given me old exams to study and I memorized them to pass the written exam which you could only miss six, and I only got four wrong. They gave me a piece of paper as a permit to drive and said the real driver's license would arrive via mail from thirty to ninety days. I came out of the DMV shocked at how easy it is to acquire basic things like a driver's license when you have everything in order, and now I could apply anywhere without breaking the law in any way or being scared of deportation.

Having lived in Mexico as tragically as it was the way it was done was probably one of the best experiences I ever had. I learned a lot about the Mexican culture and the way it is, the main differences between the United and Mexico, things you can't really describe unless you go through them, both good and bad. It helped me understand Mexico is a great country with a lot of potential if you know how to maneuver through it and life in the US is a life not to be taken for granted.

My friends whom I'll miss while back in the states. Picture taken in Nuevo Vallarta and it includes my dearest of friends Sharon Rojas to the very left (in the green dress) and next to her are Kaila Miton and Corina Heesh. Below Corina is her husband Jaime and next to Jaime is my good friend Ismael Reyes (red shirt). In the very back is myself and to the left is my good friend Sergio throwing up the peace sign. Below me starting from the left next to Corina is Deni Schneider (brown reddish hair), Mara Salazar, a friend of Corina's, then Xochi (green shirt) then it's Alan (white shirt) and Liz (black top). At the very corner is Trinidad and his wife.